50 Years of
Indian Community
in Singapore

World Scientific Series on Singapore's 50 Years of Nation-Building

---

The complete list of titles in the series can be found at
http://www.worldscientific.com/series/wss50ynb

World Scientific Series on
Singapore's 50 Years of Nation-Building

50 Years of
Indian Community
in Singapore

Editors

Gopinath Pillai

Ambassador-at-Large, Singapore &
Institute of South Asian Studies, Singapore

K. Kesavapany

President, Singapore Indian Association

World Scientific

NEW JERSEY · LONDON · SINGAPORE · BEIJING · SHANGHAI · HONG KONG · TAIPEI · CHENNAI · TOKYO

Published by

World Scientific Publishing Co. Pte. Ltd.
5 Toh Tuck Link, Singapore 596224
USA office: 27 Warren Street, Suite 401-402, Hackensack, NJ 07601
UK office: 57 Shelton Street, Covent Garden, London WC2H 9HE

Library of Congress Cataloging-in-Publication Data
Names: Pillai, Gopinath, editor.
Title: 50 years of Indian community in Singapore / editor, Gopinath Pillai,
    Ambassador-at-Large, Singapore & Institute of South Asian Studies, Singapore.
Other titles: Fifty years of Indian community in Singapore
Description: Hackensack, NJ : World Scientific, 2016. | Series: World
    scientific series on Singapore's 50 years of nation-building
Identifiers: LCCN 2016004866| ISBN 9789813140578 (hardcover : alk. paper) |
    ISBN 9813140577 (hardcover : alk. paper) | ISBN 9789813140585 (pbk. : alk. paper) |
    ISBN 9813140585 (pbk. : alk. paper)
Subjects: LCSH: East Indians--Singapore--History. | Singapore--Civilization--Tamil influences. |
    Singapore--Ethnic relations. | Singapore--History--1965–1990. | Singapore--History--1990–
Classification: LCC DS610.25.E37 A14 2016 | DDC 305.8914/1105957--dc23
LC record available at http://lccn.loc.gov/2016004866

British Library Cataloguing-in-Publication Data
A catalogue record for this book is available from the British Library.

Foreword

by S.R. Nathan

In the book *Indians in Singapore* by Dr. Rajesh Rai, the story ends with the return of the British after World War II. We can be proud of this new publication containing a compilation of essays. I applaud these efforts behind each of them. In a single volume it provides what has happened since. It differentiates what happened in the recent past, and that which has been written, for researchers on the subject to draw from. Hopefully, it also serves as a book on Indians of Singapore in recent times. In all this, the contributors have struggles with the inadequacies of archives. They have tried to meet this inadequacy with their diligence.

This book *Fifty Years of Nation Building* with an overview of the role played by the Indian community, supplements some of the inadequacies of past publications. In a single text, the essays in it form a rich but varied tapestry of the Indian community's contributions to our nation building efforts over the past. It has turned out as a book of separate parts but of shared visions — our historical creation.

The essays, though many, are yet rich in their scope and varied in nature. There were *doers* and observers. I am sure Ambassador Gopinath Pillai found the experience of compiling this series a voyage of discovery and recognise that there are many more noteworthy stories yet to be published.

In this task, the contributors must have faced their own difficulties. They had to rely largely on secondary sources and researching would have been for them a worrying task.

Life in Singapore must have been very different, unlike in India where there was a scheduled space by caste. It may have given them the appetite and inspiration not to be limited by any scheduled space, in caste-free Singapore.

My regret is that this volume speaks nothing of the Ceylonese, who contributed immensely to life in Singapore. Geographically they may be separate, but in Singapore and Malaya they were categorised among Indians and contributed tremendously to all in Singapore.

S.R. Nathan
Sixth President of the Republic of Singapore

Contents

1

A Place in the Sun

Gopinath Pillai

In 1992, the Indian Community hosted a farewell dinner for Singapore's founding Prime Minister on his retirement as PM. The Organising Committee decided to present him with a book that captured his relationship with the Indian community during his days as head of government. The title of the book was 'A Place in the Sun'. The message we were trying to convey was that in spite of the fact Indians were less than 10% of the population, he ensured we had a meaningful role in independent Singapore. He did not do this by having a token presence of Indians in visible positions. He ensured that those he inducted into the cabinet as well as senior positions in the civil service were men of substance with strong value systems. Singaporeans accepted them not because they belonged to a minority group, but because they were competent ministers and officials who carried out their jobs fairly and efficiently.

To understand the Indian community in Singapore, one needs to understand certain basic facts about them.

Indians are not a homogeneous community. They are diversified in terms of language, culture, religion, ethnicity and social strata, a euphemism for cast. In spite of this diversity, there is a common thread that runs through the community that links them all and makes them 'Indian'.

Let me give four common characteristics of the community that together form the thread that links them.

First is their love for culture, which transcends religious and linguistic differences. Some of the best singers of classical Hindustani music that has strong religious references are Muslims. The best Malayalam singer of Hindu religious songs is a Christian. These are just a few examples of the soft cultural bonds between different groups of Indians in Singapore.

Second is their love of debate. Prof. Amritaya Sen writes about the 'argumentative Indian'. Argument is part of Indian tradition because of the belief that truth can be arrived at only by vigorous debate. Some may see this as a waste of time, but the ability to articulate effectively your point of view is seen by Indians as a great asset. Connected with this is a love of politics. An extension of this penchant for politics is also the acceptance of democracy, which comes from the tradition of age-old village assemblies called 'Panchayats', where every citizen in the village has the right to air their grievances to an assembly of their peers who will decide on what needs to be done.

The third characteristic is the community's respect for education. Hindus, who form the largest group among the Indians, perhaps have the only surviving 'Goddess of Knowledge' in their pantheon of deities. The Greeks, I believe, had a goddess of knowledge, but she has not survived. The respect for education is also strong among Christians and Muslims, which is strongly embedded in their religious institutions.

The fourth characteristic of the Indians is their religiosity. Irrespective of which religion they belong to, they take their religious duties seriously and perform them regularly. Some would say that Indians are very generous in contributing to their temples, churches and mosques, but less so for other causes.

The four characteristics of Indians I mentioned perhaps help us to understand the Indian community in Singapore.

If one goes back into the history of Singapore, the period between the end of the Second World War and independence could be divided into three segments. One would be the colonial period with a legislative council. Second would be a legislative assembly under elected Chief Ministers and the third segment started when PAP came into power in 1959 with Mr. Lee as Prime Minister, but with substantial powers still with the Colonial Secretary. In all three systems, Indians played a significant role in politics and in the trade unions. They were active not only on the governmental side, but also in the opposition leftist movements.

Indian participation in politics became less prominent when voting became compulsory and other races, particularly Chinese, became more active. There was even a danger that it would become difficult for minorities to get elected. The government then decided on group representation councils with four, five and six representatives, among whom one or two would be from minority communities. In spite of the uncertainties of getting minorities elected, the cabinet had a fair share of minorities holding office who were selected on the basis of merit. This also applied to the civil service and the judiciary. Perhaps the one event that boosted the moral of the Indian community was the election Mr. S. R. Nathan as President in 2000. The Indian community felt proud not only because a member of their community was elected President, but also he was genuinely popular across all communities. This, in a way, underscored the point that Singaporeans are generally multiracial in their outlook. This is borne out by the fact that in the last 50 years since independence, Singapore has had three Deputy Prime Ministers who were Indians and numerous minority ministers.

Moving from politics to culture, the Indian communities are even more vibrant. The Tamils, who are the largest community, have the greatest number of cultural events. The Malayalees, who number about 40,000 and are the second biggest group among the Indians, have more than twenty organisations, including religious organisations, who have at least one event a month, making them culturally a very vibrant community. Then there are the Bengalis, the Telugus, the Maharashtrians, the Punjabis, the people from the Hindi-speaking states like Uttar Pradesh, Bihar and Madhya Pradesh, the Kannadias and several others. Together, they not only create a very vibrant community, but also keep the languages and many of the practices of their home states alive in Singapore.

Perhaps the most important single event in the last year was the building of the Indian Heritage Centre in the heart of Little India on a piece of land given by the government. The major part of the funding was also done by the Singapore Government. It was officially opened by the Prime Minister on 7 May 2015. I will not go into more detail on the IHC, as there is a separate article on it written by Dr. Gauri Krishnan later on in this publication.

While the Indian community in Singapore is currently in a secure and happy position, there are challenges going forward. The main challenge pertains to integration. Hitherto, the population of Singapore generally had a common background. They were migrants who came with little and worked their way up. They respected each other for their achievements. The next phase of growth will be knowledge based and the Indian community has to ensure that they place sufficient emphasis on education and training, particularly training in the latest technology. Some sections of the community may need help in this so that they reach the national average in performance.

There is another factor that needs to be attended to in our move to achieving national integration. This pertains to the issue of language. While English is still the common language, the Chinese community is encouraged to speak in Mandarin among themselves. If Mandarin is increasingly the language used by the Chinese, who make up more than 70% of the population, it effectively becomes the lingua franca of the country. The Indian community should seriously consider acquiring a working knowledge of conversational Mandarin. Learning Mandarin should not be at the expense of learning their own language or English. Indians are good at languages, as can be seen by the large number of Indians in Hong Kong who speak Cantonese. To ensure their continued place in the sun, the Indian community must get itself fully embedded in the national fabric.

Ambassador Gopinath Pillai holds several key public appointments simultaneously. He is Chairman of the Management Board of the Institute of South Asian Studies; Ambassador-at-Large in the Ministry of Foreign Affairs since August 2008; and also Singapore's Special Envoy to Andhra Pradesh.

Ambassador Pillai was Singapore's Non-Resident Ambassador to Iran between 1989 and 2008 and also served as Singapore's High Commissioner to Pakistan.

Ambassador Pillai has varied business interests which include investments in education, logistics and information technology. He is Chairman of Snowman Logistics Ltd in India; and is also Director of AEC Education PLC, listed on AIM in London.

Ambassador Pillai is also Deputy Chairman of Ang Mo Kio-Thye Hua Kwan Hospital Limited, a non-government organisation-administered hospital for step-down care. He is a member of the Steering Committee of the Indian Heritage Centre project and Chairman of its Concept and Content Sub-committee. He has also held positions of Chairman of NTUC Fairprice Co-operative Ltd for 10 years; Trustee of NTUC Healthcare Cooperative Ltd; Director of NTUC Choice Homes Co-operative Ltd; and President of the National University of Singapore Society (NUSS). He was made a Distinguished Member of NUSS in 2011.

Ambassador Pillai has received several awards, including the Friend of Labour (NTUC 1987); Meritorious Award (NTUC 1990); Friend of MCD from the Ministry of Community Development (1998); Friend of IT from Singapore Computer Society (2001) and Outstanding Service Award (NUS 2015). The Singapore government has awarded Ambassador Pillai the Public Service Star Award (BBM) in 1999, BBM (BAR) in the 2009 National Day Awards and The Meritorious Service Medal on National Day 2015.

The Indian government conferred Ambassador Pillai with the Padma Shri award at the 2012 Republic Day.

2 Indians in the Modelling of the Global Metropolis

Rajesh Rai

Introduction

The Indian community in Singapore is the product of multiple journeys — movements dating to the founding of the British colonial settlement, which have continued to this day, 50 years since Singapore's independence. Collectively, the sojourners and settlers from the subcontinent created the basis for a small but significant diaspora that has remained influential throughout the modem city's development. In 2014, Indians comprised 9.1% (353,021) of the country's resident (i.e. citizen and permanent resident) population of 3.87 million (Singapore Department of Statistics, 2014, 39). If one is to include the non-resident number, the Indian presence on the island is substantially larger — cumulatively, about 700,000 in the total (resident and non-resident) population of just under 5.5 million (2015).

The multi-layered fabric of the Indian diaspora in Singapore has been produced by multiple trajectories of emigration across the Bay of Bengal, and this, along with the complex economic topography of the city, has informed its diversity. Viewed in ethno-linguistic terms, Tamil speakers form the largest segment of the Indian population, although the diaspora also includes sizeable numbers of Malayalam, Hindi and Punjabi speakers. Hindus comprise nearly 60%, Muslims a quarter, Christians one-eighth, and along with smaller numbers of Sikhs and Buddhists, inform the diverse religious composition of Indians here. In socio-economic terms, they have prospered in the city — the average monthly income of Indian households exceeded S$7,600 in 2010 (Singapore Department of Statistics, 2010, x) — a figure that, at the last official census, was higher than any other major ethnic community (Chinese and Malays). That said, differences in income distribution amongst Indians in Singapore are also purportedly greater than any of the other major ethnic communities (Shantakumar and Mukhopadhaya, 2008, 581–5).

While always a minority, the diaspora, over its nearly 200-year history on the island, has been, and remains, an integral part of this multicultural nation. This chapter explores the formation and development of the Indian diaspora in Singapore, with a view to explaining how Indians have contributed to the transformation of a once minor frontier colonial outpost "into a metropolis of global significance" (Rai, 2014, i). Framed on the basis of key episodes in Singapore's development — the British colonial period, the Japanese occupation and independent Singapore — the study examines the distinct and complex experience of this diaspora, marking out how, at every stage of Singapore's development, Indians have left an indelible mark on the social, cultural, economic and political life of the city.

1. Forging the Diaspora

1.1. Multiple movements, diverse roles

The very 'founding' of modern Singapore was closely connected to British interests in India in the late 18th and early 19th centuries. The search for a base east of the Bay of Bengal that was strategically positioned to safeguard the East India Company's (EIC) burgeoning India–China trade was critical in Sir Stamford Raffles' decision to establish a British outpost on the island in 1819 (Tan and Major, 1995, 1–28). The first Indians in colonial Singapore came with him — mostly sepoys of the 2nd Battalion 20th (Marine) Regiment of the Bengal Native Infantry and camp followers, who were crucial in securing the fledgling colony (Rai, 2004, 1–2). Their presence marked the beginnings of a dominant position for Indians in the defence of the colony, which continued well into the early years of the 20th century.

The rapid commercial success of Singapore and the fact that the settlement was administratively a part of British India until 1867 quickly drew traders and entrepreneurs to its shores. The first, reportedly, was Narayana Pillai, an associate of Raffles, who began his career in Singapore as a clerk in the colonial treasury, but soon after ventured into brick-making, construction and retail businesses (Rai, 2006, 177). Most Indian businessmen who ventured to the early settlement were from the Coromandel Coast, a region that had long sustained commercial linkages with the archipelago. Amongst these, the 'Chulias' — a term used for Muslims from the Coromandel Coast in early Singapore — who had established a vast commercial network that extended from the Maldives to the South China Sea, constituted, certainly until the late 19th century, the largest component. Some were affluent ship owners who were engaged in the textile, gem, cattle and spice trades, while others provided petty retail services or served as boatmen, lightermen and wharfingers on the riverine trade, a segment of the economy over which they had a stronghold in early Singapore. Also prominent were the Natukkotai Chettiars from 'Chettinad', the "pioneers of microfinancing in Asia," whose credit facilities greased the wheels of commerce in colonial Singapore (See, 2015, 28). They provided a ready source of finance for individuals and businesses that would have otherwise found it hard to secure loans from European banks, and over time also came to be engaged in the property and plantation sectors. By 1935, Chettiars were said to have invested "no less than 400 million dollars" in the Straits Settlements and the Malay States (Rai, 2014, 105). Amongst other early commercial emigrants at the colony were a small but prominent group of Parsis, who, until the mid-19th century, were heavily engaged in the opium trade. In the second half of the 19th century, they were joined by Gujarati, Sindhi and Punjabi traders from north-western India, who added to the diversity of Indian entrepreneurs in a city that, by this time, had transformed into a bustling regional entrepôt.

While businessmen arrived in Singapore independently because they had the motive and the means to cross the ocean, the procurement of Indian labour required official and private intervention. The establishment of a penal colony for transported Indian convicts in Singapore in 1825 proved to be one of the most important mechanisms through which colonial authorities were able to muster large numbers of labourers for public works. Until 1873 (when the penal settlement was closed), 15,000–25,000 Indian convicts, drawn from nearly all parts of the subcontinent and from various social groups, were transported to the Straits Settlements. Most accounts suggest that their role in the making of Singapore was immense. Effectively all the large-scale building works on the island until the late 19th century — the Horsburgh Lighthouse, St. Andrews Cathedral and Government House (now called Istana), amongst others — were produced by their hands. In 1856, Governor Blundell, in his annual report to the Indian Government, provided a glowing testimony of their impressive contributions:

> The whole of the existing Roads throughout the Island, more than 150 miles in extent, every Bridge in both Town and Country, Jetties, piers, etc. have been constructed by Convict labour ... A Church has been erected every brick and every measure of lime in which has been made and laid by Convicts and which in Architectural beauty is second to no Church in India. Powerful batteries have been erected at various points and fortifications are now in progress ... which would have been too expensive for sanction if executed by free labour ...

In addition to convict labour, other mechanisms deployed to procure labour included unregulated and regulated indenture, effective until 1910, the 'Kangani' system until 1937, and the 'labour-contractor' system, which continued even after the Second World War. Notwithstanding the exploitative characteristics of all these modes, these labourers — the majority of whom came from the Madras Presidency — proved crucial in facilitating the efficient functioning of the bustling harbour and in the development of public works, railways and transportation, construction and the plantation sector.

As evident from the above, until the mid-19th century, much of Indian emigration to Singapore was connected either to commerce or labour, along with a sprinkling of servicemen in the harbour, transportation and security sectors. From the second half of the 19th century onwards, a new layer was added to the burgeoning Indian social tapestry — the outcome of an expanding and increasingly complex colonial administration, which required more educated, especially English-educated personnel, even for subaltern positions. Local sources were insufficient due to the erstwhile lack of educational development in Singapore, and neither were English-educated Europeans keen on taking up lower-ranking positions in the administration. Educated personnel from urban centres in the subcontinent provided a recourse. Higher salaries in the Straits Settlements drew teachers, administrators, surveyors, engineers, clerks and journalists from the Jaffna Peninsula, Kerala, Bengal and the Madras Presidency. Over time, their number was added to by highly educated doctors and lawyers, who comprised the main Asian component in these coveted services in Singapore during the colonial period. Along with these professionals came Sikh policemen, albeit for somewhat different reasons. The colonial administration was keen on establishing a 'neutral' police force that they felt would be useful for controlling the 'secret societies' that were especially prevalent amongst the Chinese. Sikhs, whose 'martial prowess' had long been recognised by the British, and who had already been successfully deployed to control secret societies in Perak previously, were perceived to fit the bill. From the arrival of the 1st Sikh contingent in 1881, they would remain a key component of the police force until the advent of the Second World War.

1.2. Settlement patterns, socio-cultural life and early institutions

For the overwhelming number of early Indian immigrants, Singapore was only a transition (i.e. a place where they could find work, remit funds and then return, hopefully after accumulating some capital). The vast gender imbalance in the colonial city added to that impulse — indeed, right up until the 1920s, men comprised approximately 80% of the total Indian population. The exceptions were a small number of Muslims who married into the local Malay Muslim community and settled more permanently, giving rise to the local Jawi Peranakan population. The arrival of Indian professionals and servicemen — who were provided quarters and thus were more open to bringing over their families from the subcontinent — added to the gradual increase in the settled population in the period before the Second World War.

Notwithstanding the tendency amongst the pioneers to view the island as a temporary sojourn, there were areas that over time developed Indian concentrations, and where their religious–cultural institutions came to be established. Amongst the earliest was the locale in and around Market Street, Chulia Street, Telok Ayer and South Bridge Road — a section of the larger district on the southwest of the Singapore River that the British had in fact set aside for the Chinese population. Here Indian Muslims, mainly those from the Coromandel Coast, established the Jamae Chulia Mosque (established c. 1826), the Al-Abrar Mosque (c. 1827) and the Nagore Durgha (c. 1828–30). Likewise, the earliest Hindu shrine — the Sri Mariamman Temple (c. 1827) — was set up here. Many of the early Indians were also to be found in the vicinity of the convict colony, proximate to what is today the Dhoby Ghaut Mass Rapid Transit Station. The initial Sri Sivan Temple (officially c. 1850s, but observer accounts suggest earlier) was consecrated here; and the Benggali Mosque (c. 1825–8) (now known as Bencoolen Mosque) was established on neighbouring Bencoolen Street. From the second half of the 19th century, several Indian businesses had set up shop by the Singapore river at High Street, and an Indian concentration also emerged in the vicinity of Tanjong Pagar, where the new harbour was established, and where, at the turn of the 20th century, Indian labourers came to be engaged in the construction of the Malaya–Singapore railway.

By the late 19th century the corridor to the northeast of the city, the area in and around Serangoon Road, which is known today as 'Little India', became the most important area of Indian settlement. Initially an area with a distinct European presence, Indian dairy farmers had moved to Serangoon Road by the 1830s. They were joined by Indian ostlers and syces involved in the transportation industry and as horse-riders at the nearby 'Race Course' in the 1840s, and brick kilns employing Indian convict labour were also established here. The increase in Indian labourers in the late 19th century added to this concentration, so that by this period, the vicinity was fast emerging as an Indian 'cultural space'. The Sri Veeramakaliamman Temple (c. mid-1830s), was the earliest of several Hindu shrines established here. Mosques and Churches with a predominantly Indian fellowship also gradually dotted that landscape. Retailers catering to Indian demands — whether food, dress or worship — became commonplace by the turn of the century, as did several associations based on ethno-linguistic and cultural lines. Indeed, even caste-based distance maintenance was practiced in Serangoon Road, so much so that even Chinese retailers in the vicinity were aware of these differences. Prior to the Second World War, alongside Serangoon Road, a significant Indian concentration also developed in the northern outskirts of the island around Sembawang, Seleter and Admiralty, where they were heavily employed in British military establishments, especially the naval base, which was completed in the late 1930s.

Given their sojourning patterns, the 'openness' of the port city to flows of information and communication and the centrality of India in their consciousness, the early Indians were clearly affected by socio-political contents from across the Bay of Bengal. News from the subcontinent and elsewhere featured heavily in the Tamil vernacular press, which developed from the 1870s. This tendency for the port city's dwellers to look outwards had an impact on the nature of the socio-political organisations that they developed in the diaspora. While many early institutions tended to be formed along particularistic ethno-linguistic, religious–cultural and caste-based lines, news of broader unities developing in the Indian context were that sought to bring together all Indians regardless of their linguistic, cultural and religious differences led to the formation of the Indian Association in 1923. Although the organisation's ability to reach out to the Indian masses was constrained by its elite composition, it gradually became more effective when a 'radical' leadership that actively advocated the position of Indian labour, and was well connected to Indian political notables like Jawaharlal Nehru, came to the fore in the late 1930s. Other socio-political currents that had a significant bearing on diasporic consciousness at this time was the Dravidian Movement, which emphasised Tamil unity and propagated social and religious reform within that community. Visits by leaders from the Madras Presidency such as E.V. Ramasamy Naicker and the energy of Singapore-based leaders like G. Sarangapani were crucial in broadening the reach of the movement here.

2. The Second World War and the Indian National Army

The outbreak of the Second World War and the subsequent Japanese occupation of Singapore skewed erstwhile patterns of socio-political development in the diaspora. At the outset of the war, thousands of Indians sought to escape to the 'homeland', revealing the fragility of the connection between the colonial city and its denizens. Limitations of war evacuation efforts, alongside the racist policy of allowing 'Whites' to board departing ships first, ensured that the majority of Indians would remain. For them, like the other 'races' in Singapore, the occupation was a nightmare — marked by the constant fear of Japanese brutality, and of suffering from economic deprivation and from involvement in forced labour projects.

Yet for the Indians, the occupation was also significant for another reason, as the island became the headquarters "of political and military activities for overseas Indians aiming to free ... [India] from British rule" (EID, 2006, 181). That specific role developed as Japanese wartime ambitions of removing the British from the East converged with the 'homeland' nationalist undercurrents in the diaspora. The result was the organisation of the Indian Independence Movement in East Asia, comprising the Indian National Army (INA) and the Indian Independence League (IIL), both of which were established in Singapore shortly after the British capitulation in February 1942. That movement reached its epitome under the leadership of the renowned Indian nationalist, Subhas Chandra Bose, who arrived in Singapore in July 1943. Subhas' charisma, oratorical skills and sensitivity to difference succeeded in drawing a hitherto unseen level of Indian unity across ethno-linguistic and religious lines. Beyond former British Indian soldiers, Subhas succeeded in inspiring civilians from all Indian communities to participate heavily in the movement, whether as soldiers in the INA or as functionaries of the IIL. While the outcome of the INA's attempt to attack eastern India via Imphal proved a catastrophe on the battlefield, it did play a significant role in fomenting opposition to British rule in India after the Second World War.

3. New Exigencies

The period of extraordinary pan-Indian nationalist sentiment evident during the Japanese occupation dissipated after the British arrival in late 1945. This was partly a response to the rapid collapse of the movement, but was also due to concerns of reprisals after the War. Nevertheless, the occupation had forever transformed the people of the port city. Hardened by the experience, a new generation emerged that recognised the fallibility of the British Empire. For them, the terms of the pre-war colonial order were no longer acceptable. India gaining her independence in 1947 was a source of pride for the diaspora, but that success rather than generating, enervated 'homeland' nationalist sentiments. New exigencies had come to the fore, in which local issues featured more prominently. Anti-colonial nationalism and labour assertiveness spread in Singapore and Malaya in the late 1940s and 1950s. These movements drew support from sections of the Indian community, with C.V. Devan Nair figuring prominently in the trade union movement. Other notable leaders with a socialist bent included the journalist S. Rajaratnam, who went on to become one of the founder members of the People's Action Party in 1954.

That said, the influence of 'homeland' politics did continue, albeit in a different guise. Dravidian consciousness gained popularity amongst Tamils, who comprised the majority of the Indian population. In the aftermath of the War, G. Sarangapani, publisher of the main Tamil newspaper in Singapore (*Tamil Murasu*), revived several Tamil organisations that had become defunct. He also initiated the formation of the Tamil Representatives Council (TRC) in 1951, bringing together various Tamil organisations under a common umbrella. During this period, the TRC joined hands with the Singapore Dravida Munnetra Kazagham (SDMK) to organise the popular Tamils Festival and the annual Pongal Festival (Solomon, 2012, 278), which drew considerable support. Links were forged across religious and caste lines, for example with the Tamil Muslim community and the Chettiar Chamber of Commerce. These networks enabled the TRC to act as a powerful lobby pressing for government support of Tamil language education and demanding Tamil leadership over organisations that represented Indians. Possibly the most significant achievement of such mobilisation was the recognition of Tamil as one of four official languages in Singapore in 1956, a decision that would have far-reaching consequences on the national policies that would follow. The TRC also established connections with trade unions — such as the Federation of Trade Unions and the Singapore Trade Union Congress — through leaders such as G. Kandasamy and P. Veerasenan. Their networks in turn enabled a wider role by offering grassroots support to political organisations such as the People's Action Party, in turn facilitating "the formulation of policies that favoured the Tamil-speaking sections of the Indian community" (Solomon, 2012, 279) after the party came to power in 1959.

4. Independent Singapore

Singapore was granted full internal self-government in 1959, and became independent in 1965 after a failed merger with Malaysia. Since independence, the country has witnessed "unparalleled political stability, dramatic economic growth and diversification, extensive urban renewal and the implementation of a significant social welfare programme" (Rai, 2006, 185) for all its citizens. The development of the Indian community in the wake of the dramatic transformations in Singapore over the last 50 years can be better understood in two phases: one extending from approximately 1965 to 1990 and the other from the 1990s onwards.

4.1. 1965–1990

In the first phase, one of the key changes vis-a-vis the preceding period was the development of a more settled Indian population. A series of increasingly restrictive migration ordinances put in place from 1952 to the immediate post-independence period made it difficult to continue prevailing sojourning patterns. Indians were faced with a choice — become Singapore citizens or return to India — since the new controls limited the possibility of immigration to a very small number. In this regard, TRC representatives were crucial in urging Tamils to take up Singapore citizenship, positing that they and their families were better placed here than in India. Notwithstanding these efforts, many Indians did in fact exercise the option of return, or used their position as part of the Commonwealth to move to newer pastures, especially after the closure of the British naval base in

1968, where many were employed. Consequently, the proportion of Indians in the Singapore population declined after independence, from approximately 9% in 1957 to 6.4% in 1980, before gradually increasing to 7.1% in 1990. This was, however, a far more settled population, with the gender imbalance gradually levelling from 226 Indian men to 100 Indian women in 1957 to 118 to 100 by 1990.

A significant challenge facing the government after independence was the integration of its citizens — a matter of concern given the multiracial composition and transient nature of large segments of the population. For this purpose, the state utilised campaigns, public schools, institutions and compulsory military service for men to foster national consciousness. The government also desisted from any majoritarian impulse, adhering to meritocratic principles visa-vis institutions under state control. State welfare provision did not take the form of 'handouts', but provided relatively low-cost public education and health facilities, and most importantly low-cost housing through Housing Development Board (HDB) flats in the new residential estates that began to dot the island's landscape. Indeed, by the 1990s, approximately 80% of the population were living in HDB flats, which were overwhelmingly self-owned. Quotas that emphasised a multi-racial mix in every HDB flat also acted against the formation of racial ghettoes in public housing, which in turn also had the effect of diluting erstwhile Indian residential concentrations in areas such as Serangoon Road.

The outbreak of racial riots in the 1960s left a deep impression on the government, ensuring that it exercised vigilance on polarising racial and religious 'communalism' after independence. That said, the construction of the Singaporean identity that followed did not ignore the rich racial, religious and linguistic heritage of its people. Ethnic affiliations, especially of the three main 'races' — the Chinese, Malays and Indians — were recognised as the essential building blocks of a Singapore identity. An Indian language — Tamil — was recognised as an official language and the Hindu festival Deepavali was demarcated as a public holiday. The cultivation of a Singaporean identity that embraced its own specific form of multiculturalism — labelled as CMIO, short for Chinese, Malays, Indians and Others — proved largely successful in transforming the Indian population into Indian–Singaporeans in the decades after independence.

Politically, Indians came to be well represented in government, a position that has continued to exist. Since independence, the Republic has had two presidents and numerous cabinet ministers from the Indian community. Indians also benefitted from Singapore's extraordinary growth in the 1970s and 1980s. By 1990, the average annual income of Indians in Singapore had risen to over US$10,000, and they comprised a sizeable proportion of the professional, technical and managerial segments of the economy. The Indian community also made a considerable mark on sectors such as law, and came to be well represented at all levels of the civil service. Another notable feature in the economic development of the Indian community after independence was the considerable addition of Indian women to the workforce. While Indian women comprised less than 3% of the total Indian labour force in 1957, more than half of all Indian women had come participate in the formal economy by 1990.

One of the key issues affecting the Indian community in the post-independence period pertained to the development of Indian languages. Tamil benefitted considerably from official recognition and from the policy of bilin-gualism adopted in public schools, which ensured the inclusion of the language in the national curriculum. Consequently, literacy in Tamil gradually increased to 60% of the Indian population in 1980, and the language was offered as a subject in well over 200 public schools by 1994. Furthermore, government assistance also enabled the sustenance of Tamil television and radio channels. On the other hand, the adoption of Tamil as the prescribed second language for Indians remained a cause of concern for Indian communities whose mother tongue was not Tamil. Consequently, most North Indians took up the study of Malay instead of Tamil as a second language, due to the perception that the former was easier to learn and more useful for inter-ethnic communication. However, because children from these communities were required to study two foreign languages in the curriculum, their hold over their own mother tongue diminished over time.

Another issue that had arisen by the 1990s was the decline in Indian students' performance in technical subjects — specifically mathematics and science at the secondary and pre-university level. This was not only impeding their progress at these levels, but was also leading to fewer Indian students taking up engineer-ing and science at the tertiary level, opting instead for the arts and law degree courses. Concern in this regard was a major factor informing the establishment of the Singapore Indian Development Association (SINDA) in 1991. Since its found-ing, SINDA, which is supported largely by voluntary contributions drawn from the salaries of employed Indians, has developed a comprehensive educational and welfare programme for the resident Indian community.

4.2. 1990–2015

One of the most remarkable changes since the 1990s has been the substantial increase in the number migrant Indian professionals arriving in Singapore, which has transformed the size and the socio-economic profile of the community here. That development was in part the outcome of a sharp decline in the birth rate that resulted in a rethinking of erstwhile immigration policies in Singapore by the late 1980s. The turn towards welcoming large numbers of talented individuals, especially from China and India, was added to by the imperatives of economic restructuring and Singapore's bid to sustain its competitive edge in leading industries. In 2005, the signing of the Comprehensive Economic Cooperation Agreement (CECA) Singapore and India, covering labour migration in addition to trade in goods, services and investment, further accentuated the flow of Indian professionals and businesses to the island. Consequently, as mentioned at the beginning of this chapter, the Indian population has increased substantially over the last 25 years. There is evidence to suggest considerable progress in the socio-economic profile of the community over that period. The percentage of Indians with tertiary education increased from 4.1% in 1990 to 35% in 2010, considerably higher than the national average of 22.6% (Singapore Census, 2010). Likewise, the average annual income has also increased sharply to $91,200.

While these statistics paint a rosy picture of the contemporary Indian community in Singapore, they do not account for significant issues that have arisen from changes in the demographic and socio-economic profiles of the community. There exists a general perception that the disproportionate increases in the educational profile and income are largely products of relatively recent immigration, and that comparatively long-term Indian residents and their children have not fared as well. In addition, the considerable number of migrant Indian professionals has also skewed the erstwhile ethno-linguistic profile of the Indian community, giving rise to concerns over identity. Recent sociological research suggests that resentment does exist between the so-called 'old' and 'new' diaspora. That said, the arrival of migrant professionals has been advantageous to certain sections of the 'old' diaspora, particularly those from the minority non-Tamil communities. Many Indian languages, such as Hindi, Punjabi, Bengali, Urdu and Gujarati, which had nearly vanished in Singapore in the 1980s, are now making a significant comeback. Their position has been bolstered by the new stream of migrants, as well as by changes in education policies since 1990s, which have allowed these languages to be incorporated as examinable subjects in the national curriculum.

Rajesh Rai is Deputy Head and Associate Professor at the South Asian Studies Programme, National University of Singapore. His research interests are in the area of diaspora studies, nationalism and the postcolonial history and politics of South Asia. Author of *Indians in Singapore, 1819–1945: Diaspora in the Colonial Port City* (Oxford University Press, 2014), he has also edited several major works on the South Asian diaspora including *The Encyclopedia of the Sri Lankan Diaspora* (with Peter Reeves and Hema Kiruppalini, 2013); *Religion and Identity in the South Asian Diaspora* (with Chitra Sankaran, 2013); *South Asian Diaspora: Transnational Networks and Changing Identities* (with Peter Reeves, 2009); and *The Encyclopedia of the Indian Diaspora* (with Brij Lal and Peter Reeves, 2006). Rai's articles have been published in premier academic journals such as *Modern Asian Studies, South Asia: Journal of South Asian Studies, Journal of Southeast Asian Studies* and *South Asian Diaspora*. He has a passion for teaching and has received several teaching awards at NUS. When he manages some "free time," he enjoys playing chess.

3 Singapore's Indian Heritage Centre: Curating and Negotiating Heritage, Diversity and Identity

Gauri Parimoo Krishnan

Background

The first heritage institution in the Asia-Pacific region to showcase the Indian community's heritage in multi-cultural, multi-ethnic Singapore, which comprises many migrant communities from the Indian subcontinent, was opened on 7 May 2015 by the Prime Minister of Singapore, Mr. Lee Hsien Loong. This project is largely funded by the Singapore government with a significant contribution by the Indian community, costing around 21 million Singapore dollars to build it and fit it out.

This heritage institution is conceived of as a focal point for the South Asian community living in Singapore and to develop it into a sustainable destination of cultural and historical significance for locals and visitors. Through museum excellence, its key objectives are: to connect and collaborate with key stakeholders to promote Indian culture and community rootedness; to conduct research to promote a deeper understanding of the IHC and its values; and to establish strategic partnerships with regional and international counterparts.

My association with this project started even before its inception. Sometime in 2007, I was asked to prepare a concept paper by the then-President of Singapore, Mr. S.R. Nathan, possibly because I was responsible for the development of the South Asian collection and gallery design of the Asian Civilisations Museum since its inception in 1993 and Mr. Nathan had visited the museum on several occasions. Therefore, to conceptualise the storyline for this museum and to develop its collection seemed like a natural corollary. I supported the initial development milestones of this project since 2009, from master planning, collection and storyline development, to preparing tender papers, and finally was appointed as its director in 2011 to lead a small team of curators, specialists, consultants and project managers. The journey in realising this project from planning papers and shop drawings to brick and mortar to final fit-out of showcases and gallery lighting has been phenomenal. It was a gargantuan task.

In 2009, the National Heritage Board (NHB) signed Memoranda of Understanding with representatives from the Chinese, Malay and Indian communities to provide its management and professional expertise to three Heritage Institutions in areas such as operations, curatorial support, programming and marketing.

The repositioning of the three Heritage Institutions was conducted under a co-funding framework between the Government and the three communities. It entailed the appointment of the NHB as the operator of the three institutions in order to raise the standards of these institutions to those of the national museums under the Heritage Institutions division of the NHB.

The IHC project has been steered by a Steering Committee and three sub-committees each overseeing Building and Construction, Concept and Content and Fundraising, which remained actively involved in the project for more than 5 years. The project has been steered by very insightful and passionate Indian ministers who led the project to fruition as the chairmen of the Steering Committee — at the initial stage, all of the groundwork was done under the supervision of the late Dr. Balaji Sadasivan (Minister of State, Ministry of Information, Communications and the Arts and Ministry of Foreign Affairs), who also facilitated the dialogue with the community, and subsequently, after Dr. Sadasivan's sad demise in 2010, the second minister in the Prime Minister's office, Minister for Trade and Industry and Minister for Home Affairs Mr. S. Iswaran led, guided and supported the team at various critical junctures and set high standards for its displays, interactives and the overall narrative. At various stages of the project, dialogue and feedback sessions were organised in which the community was given updates on how the IHC's collection and gallery design was shaping up, and their feedback was received and incorporated wherever possible. These dialogues were led by the chairman of the Concept and Content committee Ambassador Gopinath Pillai, deputy chairman Ambassador K. Kesavapany and members. On the building development, Ambassador R. Jayachandran, deputy chairman Ashvinkumar and members of the Building and Construction committee were deeply involved in steering the construction timeline, the quality of structure and the finishes, as well as providing critical and timely advice for improvement. Many of their suggestions were taken on board by the IHC project team that worked tirelessly to incorporate all that they possibly could. The overall management of this project was overseen by two NHB CEOs — Michael Koh and Rosa Daniel (DS, MCCY); and the Ministry of Culture, Community and Youth's Development team led by Ang Boon Yee and Elaine Go, with external consultants and contractors who tracked the timeline and budget and ensured good governance at every stage of the project. Further support and timely guidance was given by the NHB procurement and finance teams and the Group Director for Policy, Alvin Tan who oversaw the development of all the Heritage Centres.

During the period of the Centre's development, the IHC team continued to organise off-site exhibitions and programmes to generate public awareness about the Indian community's contribution to colonial and modern Singapore, as well as to connect and collaborate with key stakeholders, such as community veterans, academics, community organisations, Indian Activity Executive Committees, community centres, stakeholders in Little India, cultural associations, as well as Indian arts and heritage practitioners from various fields. The Education and Programmes team of the IHC began to incorporate audience development and engagement from mid-2013, while the curatorial team organised two very popular site-specific exhibitions — Adoring Vishnu: Vaishnava Traditions in South and Southeast Asia (2011); and Our Indian Forefathers and their Trades in Singapore (2012).

IHC Building Design Concept

The iconic four-storeyed IHC building at the junction of Campbell Lane and Clive Street in what is called the Little India Heritage District by the Urban Redevelopment Authority in Singapore embodies IHC's vision, for it blends both traditional Indian as well as modern architectural elements in its design, as defined by the original design brief. While planning this building to house the South Asian cultural heritage of 'Singapore Indians', steering clear of leaning towards any particular culture or religion of South Asia meant planning as futuristic and as contemporary a building

Fig. 3.1. Indian Heritage Centre building's lit up facade showing the facade mural against its historical and contemporary urban context of Little India. (Image courtesy of Indian Heritage Centre.)

as possible — the present design that made it to the winning stage was unanimously voted for. The concept design submitted by architects Robert Greg Shand Architects and UrbnArc Pte Ltd won the competition organised by the Singapore Institute of Architects on behalf of the NHB in 2011.

The IHC building is a green mark GoldPlus building that has undergone stringent scrutiny and follows the Building Construction Authority's guidelines for green buildings in Singapore. During the master planning stage of this project, all museological and architectural requirements, spaces and their uses were defined and articulated by the NHB and IHC teams in collaboration with CPG architects. The architectural design for the façade of the IHC is inspired by the *baoli* or *vavdi* (Indian stepped wells usually found in the western Indian states of Gujarat, Rajasthan and parts of north and central India) layout, which is covered with a glass curtain that creates an urban space inspired by geometric patterns through the arrangement of steps in wells and water tanks. This layout also alludes to the communal living and community gatherings around a *baoli* space evoked in the building of the IHC, which is representative of the South Asian community in Singapore. Its grand portal entrance is inspired by the *gopuram* gateways of the Tamil Hindu temples of Singapore and is a bespoke architectural marvel that was hand carved in Mahabalipuram from Burmese teak wood and black granite. The intricate patterns employed in the surface decoration are inspired by vegetal motifs of Tamil Nadu temples of the Chola period, Gujarati stone carvings of the Solanki period and Muslim architecture of the Sultanate and Mughal periods, thus creating a distinctive but composite style unique to the IHC.

The diversity and multi-faceted nature of Indian culture is also captured in the use of a translucent shimmering façade to create the impression of the IHC as a 'shining jewel' in the day, and the transformation of the IHC into a 'glowing lantern' of the Indian community with the lighting of the colourful façade mural at night. The unusually large mural of a photomontage, covering 50 metres in height and over 20 metres in width, captures many iconic and historic buildings associated with the Indian community, photographs of individuals and families, artefacts from the collection of the IHC and road signs with names of historic Indians who have contributed immensely to Singapore. This mural offers a snapshot of what beckons inside the centre's permanent galleries.

IHC's Gallery Content

Before the visitor goes through the galleries, a 10-minute conceptual film looping in English and Tamil provides a quick chronological overview of the Indian community's heritage in Singapore, Malaya and Southeast Asia. The film introduces five themes covered in the centre's storyline, which trace the histories, progress and achievements of the South Asian diaspora in Singapore. Arranged in five

Fig. 3.2. A view of the Introduction film with hosts representing the diversity of the South Asian community in Singapore. (Image courtesy of Indian Heritage Centre.)

vignettes that invite visitors to reflect on the five themes of the IHC's permanent galleries, each of the themes is introduced by a host character who narrates historical events and happenings. This conceptual film unfolds with a collage of archival photographs, sounds and film footage edited together with contemporary music and dance to lend authenticity and a creative edge. Inspired by the traditional Indian theatrical format of storytelling with a *sutradhara* (storyteller or a narrator), this film takes the narrative forward with a narrator for each scene, intertwined with dance and archival images. It adds an element of surprise when, from the static 'visuality' of a photograph, a character suddenly 'comes alive', lending a 'performative' interlude that brings many photographs to life and carries the narrative forward. An evocative background score created with the storyline in mind by world-renowned composer-vocalist Shankar Mahadevan provides a nostalgic and soul-stirring mood. The 10-minute score reflects the multicultural aspects of Singapore, and fuses pan-Asian traditional and contemporary sounds in order to capture the essence of each theme and its visual narrative.

This summary film contextualises the various themes dealt with in the galleries — starting with an exploration of the contact with Southeast Asia through trade and religion, to the arrival of merchants and communities in Malaya from the 15th century, to European colonisation during the 18th and 19th centuries. The 20th century focuses on the contributions of early pioneers and institutions, while the last theme reflects on the significance of on-going contributions from individuals to various sectors since Singapore's independence.

The IHC permanent galleries are located on two levels and are navigated through the *baoli* steps, which creates a unique experience of interaction between the sights and sounds of Little India against the backdrop of the historical displays and media technology. In time to come, a heritage trail will also be available for visitors to take a self-guided tour of the precinct.

- **Theme 1: Early Contact: Interactions between South and Southeast Asia**

  1st century CE–19th century

  The first gallery sets the stage by introducing a map of Indian Ocean countries and how South Asia traded with West, East and Southeast Asian countries. Archaeological finds of the 7th–9th centuries from Kedah, in Bujang valley, Malaysia and 14th century finds from Fort Canning Hill and Old Parliament House in Singapore illustrate the interactions between South and Southeast Asia in pre-colonial and colonial periods to set the stage to visually illustrate how South Asians have had long and uninterrupted communication in the region through trade, religion and other diplomatic means. It serves as a preamble to the Singapore experience of Indian migrants, establishing their long and unin-terrupted association in the broader context of Southeast Asia in the 19th and 20th centuries. Exchanges between the regions in terms of religion and trade in the pre-modern, colonial and modern era are explored in this gallery. One

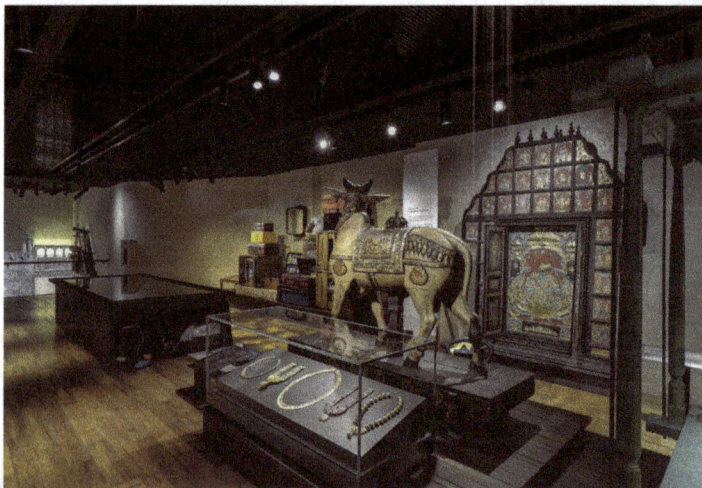

Fig. 3.3. General view of the Roots & Routes gallery with Nandi bull, temple jewellery as well as Tanjore painting of goddess Meenakshi. (Image courtesy of Indian Heritage Centre.)

such instance is the constant juxtaposition of South and Southeast Asian Hindu–Buddhist icons, Ramayana- and Mahabharata-related performing arts material as well as Islamic and Christian materials, bringing to the fore their respective and perhaps mutually inspired stylistic repertoires. There are also examples of rare Indian painted and dyed textiles that were produced in Gujarat and the Coromandel Coasts, carved wooden furniture, silverware and ivory carvings that were traded to Southeast Asia.

- **Theme 2: Roots and Routes: Origins and Migration**

19th century–21st century

Indians in Singapore and Southeast Asia trace their origins to numerous waves of migration — pre-colonial, colonial and post-colonial. A complex history of migration has produced a vibrant and dynamic community, made distinct by their ability to adapt and integrate with local cultures. The Roots section of this gallery highlights their rites of passage, attire, language, religious paraphernalia, festivals and architecture. The Routes section recreates the journeys by ship to Singapore. Through a large multi-touch interactive map inspired by Google Earth, this gallery also draws attention to the diverse places of origin of Singapore's Indian community in order to introduce their own roots and heritage to younger

Fig. 3.4. PM Lee Hsien Loong, Ministers S. Iswaran and Lawrence Wong along with invited guests taking a tour of the Early Pioneers gallery with the director Dr. Gauri Krishnan. (Image Courtesy of Ministry of Communications and Information.)

audiences. This interactive was developed with inputs from the community to validate the information as well as to encourage multi-generational interaction between community members, families and school students.

- **Theme 3: Pioneers: Early Indians in Singapore and Malaya**

  19th century–mid-20th century (pre-World War II)

  The establishment of the Straits Settlements of Penang, Malacca and Singapore (1786–1824) was followed by a steady influx of Indians from the subcontinent — from mainly Madras and Calcutta — which began with 120 soldiers of the Bengal Infantry who accompanied Sir Stamford Raffles in 1819. Among the early eminent Indians were Sangara Chetty, Naraina Pillay, Mohamed Hassan and Mohamed Lebar, who were appointed as counsels to manage the Indians by William Farquahar in 1822. From then, Indians arrived in diverse capacities, either under the auspices of the colonial government or otherwise and settled in Singapore and Malaya. This gallery showcases the various professions pursued by Indians, ranging from soldiers, convicts and plantation labourers to money lenders, businessmen, armed personnel, traditional craftsmen and artists. Through an interactive timeline, the role of the early institutions established by the community and pioneering individuals, the assertion of identity in the 19th century is reflected.

- **Theme 4: Social and Political Awakening of Indians in Singapore and Malaya**

  Mid-20th century

  In the first half of the 20th century, communities from the Indian subcontinent continued to have strong political, sentimental and economic ties with their home country and saw themselves as sojourners. Many of them returned when the First World War broke out. Many of them were inspired by the Indian Nationalist movement and followed leaders such as Mahatma Gandhi's call for freedom from British colonialism. This gallery reflects on the impact of nationalist and sub-ethnic nationalist movements on the Indian community in Malaya and Singapore; their responses to such dissemination through print and broadcast media; their interactions with visiting leaders; and their participation in the Indian National Army. Furthermore, this gallery also brings to the fore reformist activities and the revitalisation of the Tamil language and identity by leaders of the community, such as Thamizhavel G. Sarangapany.

Fig. 3.5. General view of the Indian National Army display along with Netaji Subash Bose's bust and a uniform. (Image courtesy of Indian Heritage Centre.)

- **Theme 5: Making of the Nation: Contributions of Indians in Singapore**
  Late 1950s–1980s

  This gallery showcases the contributions of Indians to the making of Singapore as a modern nation from 1945 onwards, and even more so since 1965. This gallery allows visitors to engage with artefacts, audio and video interviews, photo albums and other ephemera from the personal collections of over 180 pioneers. This gallery will continue to grow and will be updated as more pioneers are recognised in the future for their contribution to sectors ranging from business, politics, culture, to community work.

  Much of the content in the IHC galleries is also conveyed through interactives and multi-touch IT-based displays in its galleries in order to communicate content that cannot be accommodated within the limited physical space of the galleries, as well as to make the content relevant to technology-savvy younger audiences. There is a large interactive map that presents the migration of communities, a large interactive timeline that captures information about many Indian organisations and early pioneers and an interactive game of four precincts associated with Indians and how they have grown over time from 1900 to 1970. The IHC also offers visitors an immersive and novel experience with an augmented reality-enabled audio guide, which has options for child versions, adult versions and augmented reality for the visitors to select from.

Fig. 3.6.   General view of the Nation in the Making gallery with a photomontage of modern pioneers and a display of their memorabilia. (Image courtesy of Indian Heritage Centre.)

Community Contribution to the IHC

The IHC received major cash donations under the leadership of its Fundraising Committee chairman Mr. S. Chandra Das for its construction from the Harilela Hotels group, Reliance Asset Management, Adani Global, B.K. Modi Smart Group's Armorcoat Technologies and Mr. R. Jayachandran, the Chairman of the Building and Construction Sub-Committee.

The key contribution of Singapore's South Asian community to the IHC is through the sharing of tangible as well as intangible heritage. Without these, the entire storyline and visual experience of the museum would have been impossible to achieve. The IHC team has been successful in garnering support from the community who have come forward to loan or donate 368 artefacts, of which 203 are on display. A total of 443 artefacts are on display at the IHC, and 114 are on display for the first time from the NHB's national collection. More than 50 community veterans have been interviewed by the IHC team specifically for the development of the IHC's content in general, and more than 200 have been featured in the IHC galleries for their pioneering contribution to Singapore's development and nation building.

Many families have shared their heirlooms with the IHC; some came forward on their own after reading about the IHC in the media and some responded to the IHC's Collection Drive that began in 2011. The IHC has been very fortunate in receiving a major donation of gold Kasumalai from a pioneering business family of Gnanapragasam Pillai, who migrated to Singapore from Pondicherry and established a flourishing business on Serangoon Road in the early 20th century. There is a larger collection of South Indian deity jewellery in gold, silver, ruby, diamonds and semi-precious stones that came on a long-term loan from the Saigon Chettiars Temple Trust, which has enriched the section on the roots, identity and heritage of the South Indian community in Singapore. Many of the ornaments are unique and specially crafted, being made 80 to 100 years ago for dedication to the Murugan temple in Saigon, Vietnam. These two jewellery collections amply demonstrate the distribution of the living Indian traditions and tangible heritage across the Asian diaspora of the 19th and 20th centuries.

The IHC successfully managed to secure a loan from the British Library in London of the personal objects of Bhai Maharaj Singhji, a major revolutionary leader from Punjab who was captured by the British and sent to the penal jail in Singapore in 1850, where he subsequently died. His pious and spiritual nature touched many people around him, leading to a major memorial and celebration in his memory being instituted at the Silat Road Gurudwara in 1966. Another major donation to the IHC is highlighted by the bronze bust statues of the Indian nationalist leaders of the government of India, such as Mahatma Gandhi, Pandit Nehru, Netaji Subhas Chandra Bose and Gurudev Rabindranath Tagore. These adorn the gallery on social and political awakening in the early 20th century and the response to the call for freedom from British imperialism and colonisation of India. The gift also marks 50 years of Singapore–India bilateral relations and documents how Indians living in Malaya and Singapore responded to the speeches of various leaders, especially Mahatma Gandhi, whose ashes were immersed in Singapore waters and a memorial building was built on Race Course Lane in his memory with funds donated by the Indian community in the mid-20th century. The success of the Indian National Army's organisation and attack under the leadership of the revolutionary leader Netaji Subhas Chandra Bose is also well recorded with photographic evidence and other documents at the IHC. It received a significant donation of documents, photographs and audio recordings from Singapore's sixth President, Mr. S.R. Nathan, including the copy of the Proclamation of the Azad Hind, which was actually made in Singapore on 21 October 1943. Netaji was the Head of State and had appointed a number of ministers; however, the documentation of the government's actual day-to-day functioning has not yet come to light.

The last major cash donation for the IHC's major artefact of a blue and white mosque façade from Multan was received from Mr. Shahzad Nasim of Meinhardt Group with the help of the chairman of the Concept and Content Committee, Mr. Gopinath Pillai.

Acknowledgements

The author would like to thank IHC, MCCY, and PMO for granting the permission to reproduce the images in this article.

Conclusion

The IHC hopes to continue sourcing for more artefact donations, and loans, which continue to grow since its opening, as well as support for its development from the community in Singapore and globally. This is important for it to serve its mission of being the first sustainable heritage centre for the Indian community in Southeast Asia that tells the historical saga of its forebears through exhibitions, programmes, research projects and publications. It will continue to provide a platform through partnerships for education and the appreciation of Indian culture, history and arts.

Dr. Gauri Parimoo Krishnan is an art historian and museum specialist. She is an exponent of Indian classical dance who has devoted the last two decades to the heritage sector in Singapore. She has performed extensively in India, Southeast Asia and Russia during the Festival of India in the 1980s and early 1990s. Her major contributions to South Asian Diaspora Studies and Museology is the development of the Indian Heritage Centre (IHC), supported by the Singapore government and the Indian community from inception to fruition between 2007 and 2015. She planned its storyline, led teams of curators and designers in collection development, gallery and media design as its lead curator and centre director which she completed successfully in May 2015. Prior to IHC, she was the lead curator of the South Asian collection from its inception in 1993 and developed the South Asian galleries at the Asian Civilisations Museum (ACM), Singapore that opened in 2003. During her 17 years with the ACM, she has curated many block-buster and seminal exhibitions. She was also the guest curator of the NUS Museum's south Asia collection at its opening in 2002. She has a PHD in art history and a master's degree in Dance from the M.S. University of Baroda, India where she taught Art History and Aesthetics before moving to Singapore. She has authored and edited many books and articles on Indian architecture, sculpture, textile, dance and modern art. She recently published with D.K. Printworld *The Power of the Female: Devangana Sculptures on Indian Temple Architecture*. Gauri is a recipient of the Singapore government's Commendation Medal and Public Administration Medal (Bronze) for her contribution to the arts and heritage sector. At present, Gauri is the director for Fellowship & Research at the National Heritage Board's Culture Academy.

4 Little India: 50 Years of Being and Doing 'Indian' in Singapore

Nirmala Srirekam Puru Shotam

In the 50 years since the establishment of the Republic of Singapore, 'Indian' has been a word spread and repeated — and thus shared as a common-sense word. It is one of the four motifs — 'Chinese/Malay/Indian/Other' (CMIO) — that are used to talk about (the self as one of) the people of Singapore. This paradigm involved a process of institutionalisation, and was used more stringently up until the early 1990s.

The CMIO model has encountered changes that have made it more flexible. That is, it holds daily accessed meaning within the condensed words that signify Singapore's character. In doing so, it is different from what it was at the start of its emergence and institutionalisation, but it also survives as a habitual common-sense model used in conducting everyday life here.

Little India is an area that refers to the 'Indian' of the CMIO paradigm. It is a geographical space in which the numerical minority of the 'Indian' is markedly visible. The area's 'Indian' roots go as far back to the 1820s. With independence and the establishment of the Republic of Singapore, it has been highlighted for its unique stability, having been marked out as a conservation site in the 1980s and having a history associated with the 'Indians' since the 1820s.

Just as importantly, the area reflects the fact that from just before the Japanese occupation of Singapore, and into its first three decades as a Republic, immigration to Singapore was largely curtailed. Consequently, the Singaporean 'Indian' largely constituted persons born and bred here.

As a corollary to all of the above, from 1965 to the mid-1990s, the 'Indian' of Singapore was easier to describe in terms suited to CMIO-like thinking-as-usual. She or he was predominantly 'South' Indian, Tamil speaking, more prominently Hindu and generally of the middle classes.

This bias was reflected in the core clientele and/or average regular users of Singapore's Little India. This in turn shaped the primary goods and services that were stocked in the retail stores here.

Correspondingly, and at first, Little India in the first three decades of the Republic's existence made it easy to access being and doing 'Indian'. Given the numerical size of the 'Indian' Singaporean population, goods and services that were specifically 'Indian' were not marketed across the island. It was in Little India that one easily found spice pastes, fresh vegetables, freshly ground wheat and other powders, saris, highly select books and magazines written exclusively in the Tamil script, brassware such as altar lamps and iconographic images of gods and goddesses.

What the 'Indian' thus wore or cooked or read, for instance — acts that accomplished doing or being 'Indian' — was perforce possible because of Little India. Additionally, Little India also provided the stage to do and be 'Indian' with respect to particular 'Indian' events, such as 'Indian' weddings and festivals like *Thaipusam* and *Thimiti*.

Second, in providing more readily available 'Indian' goods and services, Little India inadvertently reiterated and spread only select aspects of what was contained in the word 'Indian'. It did so because it could and did offer only a selective and narrow range of how 'Indian' could be and be done. Thus, it perpetuated not just the doing of and being 'Indian' in Singapore, but also a doing of and being that were therefore specifically 'Indian' Singaporean.

Third, Little India was a powerful symbol of place and space for the 'Indian' in the model of Singaporean multiracialism. The evidence that Singapore was a city that importantly included the 'Indian' as one of its major 'races' was unquestionable because of Little India. It gave the area not just utilitarian and material value, but also one that was emotionally symbolic. For its core and regular users, this was an 'Indian' *community space*.

In contemporary Singapore, especially since the mid-1990s, the configuration of the 'Indian' has changed considerably. CMIO embraced immigrants named as 'Indian' who came from what was once British India, but now consist of the nations of India, Pakistan, Bangladesh, Sri Lanka and also a global diaspora.

The location of the new immigrants into a CMIO paradigm contrasted with at least three decades of living as 'Indian' Singaporean, and the reproducing the doing of and being 'Indian' that reflected lived experiences in Singapore's historical context. This included an at least three decades long continuity with respect to the character of Little India and its place as a community space for the average 'Indian' Singaporean. It should also be noted that the numbers of 'Indian' Singaporeans made for a space that engendered social interactions of the face-to-face kind: the population density alone has become impossible for such to occur in Serangoon Road in contemporary times.

Thus, by the mid-to-late 1990s, Little India had changed considerably. The first powerful impact upon it was the preponderance — at certain times of the day and throughout Sundays — of 'Indian' foreign workers. Local-born 'Indians' avoided the area at these times. 'Little India' was no longer available at any time of any day for the Singaporean 'Indian'.

The 'Indian' worker influx reflected an earlier government policy to obtain labour from 'traditional' sources. The most prominently recognised 'Indian' foreign workers visible and catered to in Little India are the Tamil and Bangladeshi workers.

'Indian' immigrants into British Singapore had, indeed, been drawn primarily from the Madras and Bengal Presidencies of British India. The Madras Presidency in the Republic of India comprises a variety of states in the Republic of India today, a major one of which is Tamil Nadu. The Bengal presidency has been divided into a state of India — Bengal — and a separate nation — Bangladesh.

Little India as a community space has reinvented the British era to quite some degree. Thus, 'Indian' foreign workers who overflow the pavements and streets in the part of Little India that runs from Serangoon Road from the junction of Kerbau Road to the junction of Kinta Road are predominantly from Tamil Nadu. One hears Tamil spoken here. One finds the Hindu temples here overflowing with the presence of Tamil Hindu workers seeking solace or offering penance. Shops in this area, especially in the Kerbau Road quarter, cater to some of their needs and are even oblivious to the 'Indian' Singaporean.

From the junction of Kinta Road upwards, and especially in the area of Syed Alwi and Desker Roads, the Bengali language predominates, where the 'Indian' foreign workers spill onto the roads from overcrowded five-foot pathways. The mosques here, especially the one on the main Serangoon Road, proffers the solace that temples along this road offer to the Hindu Tamils.

These temples and mosques were once places where Hindu and Muslim shrines were situated. They reflect how the area was, from its early beginnings in the 1800s, divided into two basically Hindu and Muslim areas. The Hindu areas of Serangoon Road in the colonial period, from where the tell-tale names such as Kerbau Road and Buffalo Road come from, became prominent for the rearing of dairy animals, including cows, as labour and for their milk. The Muslim areas, especially Syed Alwi and Desker Roads, bordered what was once an area for the slaughter of cattle for meat, and the related tanning industries. While these two dominant uses of the areas have ceased altogether, these historical strata left aspects that reiterate the contemporary versions of being Hindu and Muslim, Tamil and Bangladeshi *and* 'Indian' labourers.

However, as in days of yore, division is not the only characteristic that is present. Little India also works to ensure that these flows meet and interact to find some commonality and identity. Shops on Serangoon Road, at the junction of Syed Alwi and Desker Roads, cater to the sale of products and tailoring services at prices that are affordable and attractive to the low-waged foreign workers. Remittance centres and mobile phone outlets as well as gold jewellery stores along Serangoon Road attract both groups. As in British Singapore, Race Course Road still brings diverse groups together. Where once this was because they came to watch and place bets on horse racing, the field that remains the race course is used for live and screened shows that cater to the 'Indian' foreign worker today on select and festive occasions.

As if to emphasise the whispers of an older time, amidst these two groups of people is another category of the foreign worker, akin to the categories of such in colonial Singapore. She and he come from mainland China. In contemporary times, they are here because they are hired by Singtel: 'dressed' in boards displaying script and the Singtel logo, they work as walking advertisements. They do not interact with the 'Indian' workers, not least because they do not speak the same language. Their placards, however, do. Those standing amidst the heavy flow of pedestrian traffic along Serangoon Road and before the junction with Kinta Road carry the Tamil script. Those standing past the Kinta Road junction carry boards in the Bengali script.

Their scarcity reflects the historic character of Little India. 'Chinese' in colonial times did not favour this area much. The reasons for this are complex and varied, but suffice it to say that the most prominent aspects of their presence were to be found by way of vegetable gardens cultivated particularly by Roman Catholic Teochews, and the Tan Tock Seng Pauper Hospital, which spent a better part of its time deliberating over how to practically imprison the 'Chinese' in the hospital so that they would not run back to the town. The mainland Chinese, similarly, do not cross over into this area as they would and do in Singapore's Chinatown. The discourse of the past continues in some respect the narrative of the present. Fifty years of Singapore history represent an interesting historical continuity, without which it could never have been in the first place.

By the 2000s, there came yet another prominently noticed 'Indian' immigrant: the 'Indian Indians'. This term refers to relatively recent immigrants from the Indian subcontinent or 'Indians' from a global diaspora, including the USA. As these 'Indian Indians' include those who hope to make Singapore a permanent home, they constitute the potential of becoming 'Indian' Singaporeans. Predominantly, they are also at least upper-middle class or socioeconomically far wealthier than the average Singaporean 'Indian'.

Prior to their arrival, the major 'Indian' Singaporean was already one whose life in Singapore could be traced back to a decision to immigrate into British Malaya. Their forefathers and foremothers were first-generation immigrants, while they were largely born and living as 'Indians' in Singapore for all 50 years of its existence as a republic.

The new 'Indian Indians' arrived as the potential forefathers and foremothers to their children and, perhaps even more so, grandchildren. Their Singapore is experientially more immediate. They do not carry the weight of history.

An important aspect of this is the lived experience of a time before and a time after the arrival and spread of Housing and Development Board (HDB) apartments. Resettlement into HDB estates generally brought to an end the existence of 'Indian' residential neighbourhoods. This is especially due to the HDB's policy of ensuring HDB estates reflected the CMIO ratio in the national demographic.

Accordingly, the symbolism of Little India as a community space is a facet found amongst 'Indian' Singaporeans. In 1980, when it was expected that Little India would be demolished by modernisation and development, the core clientele and regular users of the area bemoaned this possibility, even denying that it would actually happen.

A community space reflects such a valuation. The 'Indian' foreign worker also comes here for this reason. It is this perception of their need that the 'Indian' Singaporean, while grumbling about their overwhelming presence, admits empathy with. They understand that by being 'Indian', this category of foreign worker does wend its way here for reasons that are certainly understandable. There is here some sense of shared understanding that this is Singapore's Little 'India'.

In contrast, there are the 'Indian Indians' who can and do mock the area's claim to being a Little India. This is especially easy as Singapore's Little India is minute compared with the largesse that is the Republic of India. Added to this, the immigrant 'Indian Indians' come from the class of the rich and newly rich. She and he are also sharply aware of the new, global India and 'Indian Indians'.

Little India, then, is not as easily generative of sentiment and affection from 'Indian Indians'. Indeed, global 'Indian Indians' and the 'new' India lend comparisons via which Little India can be spoken about as lacking in as many areas as one can care to perceive it from.

A prime example pertains to the reading of Little India as not being the best place to buy 'Indian' clothes. The once more common sari shops that also used to line the main road are mostly gone. They did not benefit from the sudden rise in 'Indian' consumers that the 'Indian Indian' immigration could have allowed. 'Indian Indians' have, instead, seen to the proliferation of sari and other 'Indian' textile and dress sales, which they hold in private spaces and at the occasional public event. Here, they offer a greater diversity of regional textiles and saris and other clothing that is often more expensive, as well as newer designer clothing that Serangoon Road does not sell. One could also argue that because of this, these types of 'Indian' goods in Little India have themselves, therefore, become narrower, even more kitschy and have contributed to the end of some of the once more famous sari shops in the area.

At the same time, the 'Indian Indians' have to attend to those needs that enforce some degree of dependence on Little India. Simultaneously, their 'Indian' character has stimulated changes that are considered 'natural' to an area servicing the 'Indian' in Singapore. One of the most apparent examples of this pertains to the arrival, rise and proliferation of 'Indian' beauty salons. While sari shops were difficult to avoid in the first 30 years of Little India's existence in its national space, the beauty salons that offer hennaed hair, eyebrow threading and Ayurvedic and other Indian-based hair loss treatments are the new kids on the block.

With them has come the new Indian woman entrepreneur, in an area that claimed for almost 30 years the fact that women would never run 'Indian' businesses. These women openly state that such salons are due mainly to the presence of the newer 'Indian Indians'. 'Indian' Singaporeans do use the services now as well, but the path for them was carved out by the greater demand made by the former group's way of life. These salons, it should also be mentioned, could not exist without the expertise of their largely 'Indian Indian' employees.

Another example of this utilitarian interest in Little India relates to food, both in terms of the restaurants that have now diversified with respect to a larger number and variety of 'Indian' cuisines, but also with respect to everyday meals cooked in the privacy of the home.

Thus, ingredients, kitchen tools and appliances and such, without which an 'Indian' meal would be more difficult to accomplish, can be bought here. 'Indian' festivities, of which there are more now than ever before, as these reflect diverse Hindu lunar calendar readings, are often denoted by special dishes, which Little India also enables.

As noted, in the 50 years since Singapore became a nation, such material culture as that which enables the reproduction of 'Indian' food reflected the more dominant core of the 'Indian' Singaporean profile — South Indian and Tamil. The middle class narrowed the expanse of goods and services that were considered sufficient for being of and doing 'Indian' Singaporeans.

Little India of the 2000s, in contrast, is a veritable explosion of goods and services, reflecting the rise of global India. On the one hand, this has wiped out some ways of doing and being 'Indian' in Singapore. Milkmen no longer provide the milk from which a whole array of 'Indian' foods, sweetmeats and ritual activities are derived. Indeed, one does not need to buy milk from Little India, as the ubiquitous packaged milk is available in almost every supermarket. Flour and spice grinders have finally been completely erased from the area.

However, one can buy into a whole range of being and doing 'Indian' that the 'Indian' of even the first three decades of Singapore's national existence could not. An example par excellence of this relates to 'Indian' food, as can be found in Mustafa's.

Mustafa's is a veritable Aladdin's cave of 'Indian' treasures. This humongous and multi-level department store showcases — for all of 24 hours — an impossibly complex range of things that can be added to the therefore increasingly complex ways of doing and being 'Indian' in Singapore. It is the one place where one can be certain of finding the goods suited to being and doing 'Indian' as 'Indian' Singaporeans, 'Indian' foreign workers and 'Indian Indians' who are or are not Singaporean permanent residents or citizens.

A tiny glimpse of this is the range of mixtures available under the single brand 'Shan', which can substantially change the reproduction of 'Indian' meals in an 'Indian' home here. The brand offers, for example, the means to make *Sindhi Briyani, Plain Briyani, Bombay Briyani, Pav Bhaji, Lahori Fish, Achar Ghosht Curry, Meat Masala Vegetable Curry, Chicken Tikka, BBQ Mix, Chicken Curry, Channa Chaat Seasoning, Fruit Chaat Seasoning, Dahi Bara Chaat, Chaat Masala, Qasuri Methi, Fish Seasoning Mix, Chops/Steaks Mix, Chicken Roast Mix, Brain Masala Mix, Liver Curry Mix, Dal Curry Mix, Channa Masala, Meat and Vegetable Mix, Rogan Josh, Keema, Paya, Nihari* and *Dopiaza*.

In conclusion, doing and being 'Indian' in Singapore was always possible because of a road proposed to be built in 1822. This road made the area around it accessible to a largely swampy and low-lying and flood-prone area, through which ran a part of the Rochore River.

This made it a suitable site for the raising of cattle, and with that the slaughter of some of these beasts. As with public works, the cattle trade brought more 'Indian' immigrants into the area. With them came a customer base that the astute commercial migrant catered to. In particular, these were initially itinerant hawkers who sold their wares to the working classes.

As an urban centre, Singapore was not the place to which large numbers of the 'Indian' immigrants, employed in rubber estates, were deployed to, particularly from 1905 to 1938. 'Indian' immigrants to Singapore reflected the town that was central to it. They formed an important component of British Indian migrants who came as 'Indian' English-speaking clerks and other administrators; junior engineers and surveyors who worked under their British qualified equivalents and could never surpass them because of imperial codes; and the merchants and traders who saw opportunities in a world-renowned entrepôt.

They formed a class of 'Indians' in Singapore who were among the first to establish 'Indian' family life here. Family life meant the presence of 'Indina' women, the major reproducers of the 'Indian' in Singapore. Women also highlighted the need for 'Indian' products because they largely worked as unrecognised but skilled homemakers. Further, while their men switched to garments suited to the British world of work, the women stayed closer to their original dress codes and manners, as well as the activities that involved being and doing 'Indian'.

Being of the class with the greater potential and interest in spending money, they provided the impetus for the emergence and takeover of the area by commercial traders. Thus it was that the area evolved to become the space in which a particular complex of 'Indian' everyday life in Singapore was both possible and sustainable.

Little India is teeming with life and complexities, engendered by a sharp change in policies pertinent to Singapore's demographic profile. While the model of CMIO retains its habitual and hence taken-for-granted status, the meanings that are condensed within it have become considerably expanded. This has ensured intense social interactional possibilities and related negotiations that include those that can and do generate conflict. Little India showcases this as a primary space that is necessary for the doing and being 'Indian'. It clarifies that a socially valued idea of biological essentialism regarding one's race is, really, always on-going. It has to be reproduced to survive, and that reproduction is a 'tradition' that is reflective of its more immediate and historical context.

Select References

Amrith SS. (2011). *Migration and Diaspora in Modern Asia.* Cambridge University Press, New York, NY.

Buckley CB. (1902). *An Anecdotal History of Old Times in Singapore from the Foundation of the Settlement Under the Honourable the East India Company on Feb. 6th, 1819 to the Transfer to the Colonial Office as Part of the Colonial Possessions of the Crown on April 1st 1867.* Fraser and Neave, Singapore.

Koh G, Soon D, Teng YM. (2015). Introduction. In: Teng YM, Koh G, Soon D (eds) *Migration and Integration in Singapore: Policies and Practices.* Routledge, Abingdon, pp. 1–24.

Loh KS. (2007). Black areas: urban kampongs and power relations in post-war Singapore histiography. *Sojourn: Journal of Social Issues in Southeast Asia* **22**: 1–29.

Mani A. (1993) Indians in Singapore. In: Sandhu KS and Mani A (eds) *Indian Communities in Southeast Asia.* ISEAS, Singapore, pp. 789–810.

Puru Shotam N. (1992). The Singapore Indian trader. Traditions of a modern economy. In: Chong YM (ed) *Asian Traditions and Modernization.* Singapore, Times Academic Press.

Puru Shotam NS. (1998). *Negotiating Language, Constructing Race: Disciplining Difference in Singapore.* Berlin, New York, Mouton de Gruyter.

Puru Shotam N. (n.d.). *Making Space for Doing Race* (tentative working title) (In process).

Sandhu KS. (1969). *Indians in Malaya: Some Aspects of their Immigration and Settlement 1786–1957.* Cambridge, Cambridge University Press.

Siddique S, Puru Shotam NS. (2000). *Singapore's Little India. Past, Present, and Future* (1990; 2nd edition with epilogue). Singapore: Institute of Southeast Asian Studies.

Stenson M. (1980). Indian peoples in the colonial economy, 1907–1941. In: Stenson M. *Class, Race and Colonialism in West Malaysia. The Indian Case.* St. Lucia, Queensland, University of Queensland Press, pp. 14–34.

Turnbull CM. (2009). *A History of Modern Singapore, 1819–2005*. Singapore, NUS Press.

Teng YM. (2015). Immigration and Integration in Singapore. In: Teng YM, Koh G, Soon D. (eds) *Migration and Integration in Singapore: Policies and Practices*. Routledge, Abingdon, pp. 25–38.

Yeoh BSA. (2013). 'Upwards' or sideways. Cosmopolitanism talent/labour/migration in the globalising city-state of Singapore. *Migration Studies* **1**: 96–116.

Nirmala Srirekam Puru Shotam has written various books and articles, including *Negotiating Multiculturalism: Disciplining Difference in Singapore* and the co-authored the award winning *Singapore's Little India. Past, Present, and Future*. Puru Shotam's earlier career was largely with the Department of Sociology, National University of Singapore. She resigned from a tenured position as Associate Professor to work as an independent scholar. Her current projects include *Making Space for Doing Race*, an examination of the accomplishment of race-d identities, particularly with respect to the more recent immigration policies pertinent to Singapore. Her other large project at this time is *The Pink Hippo*, a series of books for children that deal with issues of difference.

5 Indian Contribution to Visual and Performing Arts in Singapore

Jaya Mohideen

Visual Arts

Indians made significant contributions to the visual arts in Singapore at a national level. At the ethnic Indian level, Indian visual arts in Singapore remain modest. The exponential developments in Chinese visual arts in Singapore emanate from the Chinese population size and the Chinese merchants and elite, clan associations, and Chinese art societies that nurtured and supported them. Several of these artists have become national icons, such as Liu Kang, Chen Wen Hsi, Cheong Soo Pieng, and Georgette Chen. By contrast, Indian merchants did not have the same passion for visual arts. They, along with the Indian elite, tended to favour Indian performing arts.

Despite these constraints, Indians have contributed to the visual arts in Singapore by transcending the Indian community and focusing on Singapore as a whole. It was principally the establishment of art institutions, notably the LaSalle-SIA College of the Arts, which spurred Indian artists to move to centre stage. The LaSalle group that emerged included S. Namasivayam, Venka Puroshothaman, Dr. S. Chandrasekaran, Kumari Nahappan, and Jeremy Sharma.

Namasivayam was a veteran art educator and mentor to many successful Singapore artists. Venka is an eminent arts veteran with extensive knowledge of Singapore's visual and performing arts. He is Vice-President and Provost of the LaSalle College of the Arts and has raised the profile of Singapore art internationally.

Chandrasekaran is renowned as an arts educator, painter, and sculptor. He has represented Singapore at major international exhibitions and seminars. Kumari has excelled as a painter and sculptor. Her landmark sculptures include 'Pedas-Pedas' for the National Museum, 'Nutmeg' at ION Orchard, 'Saga' at Changi Airport, and the 'Happy Tango' Artist of the Year Installation at the Shanghai Art Fair 2011. Jeremy merges visual art with his other passion, music. A lecturer in fine arts, Jeremy has experienced a meteoric rise as an artist, with his works exhibited at major platforms in Singapore and abroad.

Other Indians who have contributed to visual arts in Singapore include:

- Rupa Natarajan, a painter for 35 years, who has contributed to the National Arts Council and arts awareness in Singapore;
- P. Gnana whose art is principally inspired by Indian subjects and owns The Gallery of Gnani Arts;
- Ketna Patel, who is renowned for her pop art, and who has successfully used her genre in merchandise such as furniture;
- Madhvi Subrahmaniam, a writer, artist and curator who makes wondrous ceramics using a former Dragon Kiln in Jalan Bahar;
- Manjeet Shergill with her signature style of figures and landscape.

The visual arts scene would not be complete without the art galleries that have contributed to the development of the visual arts in Singapore. The notable galleries helmed by Indians are:

- Galerie Belvedere which is owned and managed by Jaya Mohideen and Rasina Rubin. Founded in 1996, the gallery promotes Singapore artists and Asian and European painters and sculptors.
- Gajah Gallery, which was established by Jasdeep Singh, exhibits and promotes works by Indian, Chinese, and Southeast Asian (including Singaporean) artists.
- Indigo Blue Art was founded by Suman Aggarwal to showcase Indian contemporary art.
- Sundaram Tagore Gallery, which is owned and managed by Sundaram Tagore. Established first in New York, the gallery's presence in Singapore has added to Singapore's international dimension as a centre for the visual arts.

In the ecosystem of the arts, an important component is formed by the writers and commentators of the arts. T.K. Sabapathy is one of Singapore's leading art historians. Trained under Michael Sullivan at the then University of Malaya (in Singapore), Sabapathy has written several books and numerous commentaries including the seminal *'Modernity and Beyond: Themes in Southeast Asian Art'*. He established and headed pioneer art research facilities in Singapore, such as the Contemporary Asian Art Centre and Asia Contemporary. He has devoted himself to the research, documentation, and support of contemporary visual arts in Singapore. He taught Art History for many years at the National University of Singapore (NUS), Nanyang Technological Institute, and the National Institute of Education. He is currently Adjunct Professor at the Department of Architecture, NUS.

The most prolific writer and art critic on Singapore visual arts is Deepika Shetty, a Senior Arts Correspondent with *The Straits Times*. For almost a decade, Deepika has developed and shaped the newspaper's coverage of the arts and has won awards for her contributions. She served at Channel News Asia as a producer and anchor, and was in SINDA for many years. In India, she worked for *The Times of India* and *India Today*. She is author of *'The Red Helmet'* and has galvanised a following for her popular Facebook page 'Sadee Saree'.

Akshita Nanda, also an arts correspondent at *The Straits Times*, reviews books, conducts interviews with renowned personalities, and writes about the visual and performing arts and special lifestyle articles on Singapore.

Performing Arts

We have a rich galaxy of stars in the performing arts. It was through music and dance that the Indian cultural identity was forged in Singapore.

A leading institution is the Singapore Indian Fine Arts Society (SIFAS), which was established in 1949. Its founder members included S.N. Dorai, K.P.A. Menon, V. Govalam, K.C. Natarajan, and Dr. E.A. Shankar. Over the past 50 years, it has gained international recognition as a centre for excellence in Singapore for Indian classical dance, instrumental music and vocal music in both Hindustani and Carnatic. SIFAS is committed to promoting Indian dance and music to non-Indians and has produced non-Indian exponents of Indian classical music. Although SIFAS started with a primary focus on Carnatic music and Bharatha Natyam, it now has a pan-Indian curriculum, taking into account the diversity of Indian languages and cultures and the multi-ethnicity of Singapore. Its Sanskrit motto 'Art Characterises Civilisation' is pertinent to Singapore. As we celebrate our 50th anniversary in 2015, there is a growing awareness that to sustain our status as a first-world country, we need to continue to embrace art in its many facets.

SIFAS has been nurtured by many performing stars, including Dr. M. Chotta Singh, Mrs. Sharada Shankar and her daughter Dr. Uma Rajan, Mrs. Rathi Karthigesu, Pandit Ramalingam, and M.V. Gurusamy. Mrs. Shankar was a pillar of strength at SIFAS. She took on the task of developing Indian classical music as a teacher and performer. In stage shows and dance performances, she was the lead violinist, often accompanying renowned musicians from India. Mrs. Shankar and A. Rajah established the first Indian orchestra in Singapore, 'Ramakrishna Sangeetha Sabha'.

Born to a family steeped in classical music, Uma had her formal music and dance training at the Indian Institute of Fine Arts, Pandanallur, Chennai. On her return to Singapore, Uma sang Carnatic songs on Radio Singapore and later on Singapore TV and performed lead roles on stage. Despite the demands of her job as Director of School Health at the Ministry of Health, Uma remained dedicated to her immense talent as a classical singer and dancer.

Dependant for decades on itinerant and peripatetic teachers and performers, SIFAS recruited Shankari Krishnan, a graduate of Kalakshetra. She was multi-talented and taught singing, dance, and the Veena. Proper curricula were established for music and dance, and examinations were set together with accrediting bodies in India.

Mrs. Rathi Karthigesu was a Bharatha Natyam pioneer in Singapore. Trained in Singapore and India, Rathi was another key pillar of SIFAS. Her strength as a dancer and performer led her to encourage and support the work of Shankari. Rathi was Vice-President of SIFAS, and her husband Justice M. Karthigesu was President, at different times. Rathi's cousin Mrs. Vijeya Lakshmi Rajah (wife of Justice A.P. Rajah) was not directly involved with SIFAS, but was invited to perform at major temple events and at public concerts organised by Dr. Chotta Singh. Mrs. Rajah was a highly accomplished singer of Indian classical music and played the Veena. Rathi's brother, Padma Selvadurai, is the current President of SIFAS and has helmed it for the past decade. Under his leadership, a key objective of SIFAS is to promote Singapore through its productions and to showcase Singapore as a regional centre for the performance and display of Indian fine arts.

Apart from SIFAS, three other schools are significant in the development of the performing arts in Singapore. The first is Bhaskar's Academy of Arts, established in 1952 by K.P. Bhaskar and his wife Santha to teach dance in Singapore and Malaya. In 1965, upon Separation, Bhaskar decided to stay in Singapore, where he contributed his talents as a dancer, teacher, choreographer, and writer. He was much involved with community work through the People's Association, the Kreta Ayer People's Theatre, and the Singapore Arts Federation.

Apsaras Arts is the second dance company that was founded by S. Sathyalingam and his wife Neila in 1977. Both were originally from Sri Lanka but met at Kalakshetra, Chennai, India. Kalakshetra, reputed to be among the best dance institutions in India, honed the talents of the gifted Sathyalingam and his student Neila. Together they espoused high standards in their teaching and the promotion of traditional Indian dance in multiracial Singapore, and they gained international recognition. Neila was bestowed Singapore's Cultural Medallion in 1989.

The third school is the Temple of Fine Arts, inspired by Swami Shantanand Saraswathi in 1981. Their belief was that by teaching the arts and offering performances, they could bring about peace and joy to those they come into contact with. They offer programmes in Indian classical music (vocal and instrumental), Indian dance styles, and yoga. They have managed to reach out to many non-Indians in Singapore by adapting non-Indian themes in their performances.

A leading Singapore-born dancer not associated with any of these schools is the Cultural Medallion winner of 1979, Madhavi Krishnan. She was a pioneer in Indian classical dance and choreography. She was trained in the classical dance traditions of Bharata Natyam under Guru T.V. Soundarajan, and Kathakali by Guru Gopinath Thangamani. She toured India and Southeast Asia, including a performance at the Victoria Theatre. In the 1960s, she was an actress in the Madras film industry due to her beauty and talent as an accomplished dancer. Madhavi realised that her home was in Singapore, despite the allure of the film industry. She returned to Singapore in 1970 and set up the National Dance Company through which she integrated classical Indian dance forms with multicultural influences. Madhavi was the principal dancer and choreographer of her company. In 1971, she choreographed 'Thaipusam' as Singapore's contribution to the Adelaide Arts Festival. Music, ballet, opera, and English language were woven by Madhavi into her works 'Meera' and the opera-inspired 'Savitri'. Madhavi performed internationally and won many accolades for Singapore.

Another renowned dancer is Sharmila Gunasingham, who is a corporate lawyer and the Managing Director of Global Law Alliance. An accomplished exponent of classical Indian dances, Sharmila's objective is to spread the universal messages of peace and enlightenment. She is known to perform and dance with famous non-Indian artistes "to break down the barriers of race and religion through the soft power of the arts."

In theatre, notable contributions have been made by Gaurav Kriplani at the Singapore Repertory Theatre (SRT), of which he is Managing Director. From a small fledgling outfit established in 1993, Gaurav has raised its stature and reputation to be amongst the best English-language theatres in Asia. Apart from main stage productions, the SRT has a 'Young Co.' as an educational and performing platform for 16–25 year olds in order to nurture young talent, as well as 'The Little Company', which produces quality plays performed by professional adult actors for young children.

This subject will not be complete without crediting the major contributions of P.S. Raman, the first Head of the Indian Section at Radio Singapore. He rose rapidly to become the Chief Executive of Radio and TV Singapore and played an important role when Separation was announced on 8 August 1965. He is credited with forging our radio and television services from the third world to first world in a short span of time. He was appointed Singapore's first ambassador to Indonesia in 1968.

In the past 50 years of nation building in Singapore, Indians have contributed significantly to the visual and performing arts at national and international levels. They have transcended their Indian community to become national players and have integrated multi-ethnic and multi-cultural influences, resulting in a uniquely Singaporean sensibility.

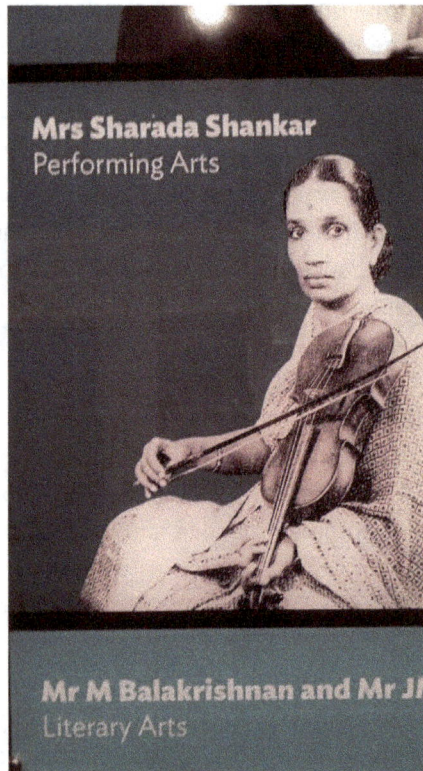

Sharada Shankar.

Rathi Karthigesu on stage with then Law Minister, Eddie Barker and Punch Coomarasamy.

Mrs. Jaya Mohideen began her career in the Singapore Administrative Service with postings to the Ministry of Defence, Public Service Commission, and Ministry of Foreign Affairs. She is the first career woman Ambassador and has served as Ambassador of Singapore to the European Union, Belgium, The Netherlands, Luxembourg, The Holy See, and the Czech Republic, and is currently Ambassador to Finland. Mrs. Mohideen was awarded the Wolfert van Borselen Medal by the City of Rotterdam in 1992. She was knighted "Commandeur of the Order of Orange-Nassau" by Queen Beatrix of The Netherlands in 1993 for promoting bilateral economic relations between The Netherlands and Singapore. She was awarded the Public Service Star by the Singapore Government in 2009.

Mrs. Mohideen has served on the Board of Trustees of SINDA, as Vice-Chairperson of the Singapore Indian Chamber of Commerce and Industry, Patron in the Tanjong Pagar GRC, President of MINDS, and Deputy Chairperson of the Public Arts Appraisal Committee under the Singapore National Heritage Board. She is married to Justice M.P.H. Rubin, retired Singapore Supreme Court Judge.

Fifty Years of Singapore Tamil Literature

Mani, A.

At the time of Singapore's separation from Malaysia in 1965, owing to the colonial past, a cultural gulf existed between English-educated Tamils and predominantly Tamil-using Tamils. Tamil literature was left to the latter to be fostered as part of their Tamil language efforts. Becoming and being a literati has been the ideal among them. This ideal was rooted in the late colonial period and fully developed in the post-colonial years in Tamil Nadu, Malaya and Singapore. Most writers were low-income earners associated with working-class Tamils. Most of them were unschooled and worked as daily rated labourers, hair-dressers, road laying coolies, port workers, Tamil school teachers and some were even unemployed. Their asset was their high aspiration to be recognised as a writer. This passion drove them to self-educate themselves in the art of writing grammatically structured poetry, short stories and novels and become eloquent public speakers. Amongst the Tamil writers of that era, those who worked at the radio stations and newspapers or at the *Indian Movie News* magazine were considered as being privileged as they were paid to write. Often, they remained a class apart from the rest of the writers.

Post-colonial Singapore, being a new nation in the making, created many new institutions as part of its state-building project. Arising from the state-led projects, the Chinese community was restructured with censorship, multi-racialism and many other projects. The Tamil language, except for its recognised status as an official language, was benignly neglected in the making of Singapore. Organisations within the Tamil community also did not adapt rapidly to face these new challenges, including the field of Tamil literary writings. While the government took the lead in defining Chinese culture and Mandarin as the language of Chinese Singaporeans, Tamil literature as well as Tamil language were left to the community's efforts to define themselves. Just as in the case of the Chinese, the hitherto dominant ethnic Tamil social mobilisation became defunct, marginalised and unable to adapt to the changing political landscape. This would be reflected in much of the Tamil writings in the post-independence years where the Tamil writers went on to write about mundane matters that were non-political, non-racial and non-of-anything that the state did not desire. All writings for radio and newspapers were devoid of social issues *per se* unless the editors viewed them as non-controversial.

Much of the recent critiques of the history of Singapore's Tamil literature easily lend themselves to listing names of writers and their contributions (see, for example, Thinnappan *et al.*, 2011). Their reflections and analyses hardly examine the institutional architecture that promoted Tamil literature in Singapore. Pre-independence, organisational structures such as the *Tamil Murasu, Tamil Nesan* (both daily Tamil newspapers), *Indian Movie News* (a monthly publication), radio stations in Malaya and Singapore and occasional publications by organisations promoted the publication (in the form of publishing and broadcasting writer's works) of poetry, short stories and dramas. There were also two contending community festivals such as the *Thamizhar Thirunaal* and *Pongal Thirunaal*, which promoted competitive writing of poetry, short stories and dramas. Both were festivals organised by organisations and power groups within the Tamil community. At the time of Singapore's independence, the *Tamil Malar, Tamil Murasu* and the Singapore radio station were the sole publishers of Tamil writings. The *Tamil Murasu* under community leader G. Sarangapany had closed down temporarily in 1963 owing to a worker's strike, and subsequently, the *Thamizhar Thirunaal* annual festival declined as it was also under the same leader. *Pongal Thirunaal* also declined with the forced name change of its major proponent *Singapoor Dravida Munnetra Kazhagam* in 1967 (see Mani, 2014). Very few writers published their written works as individual volumes owing to their meagre incomes as well as the transitional challenges faced in Singapore becoming a country and aspiring to become a nation. It was also extremely difficult to have new organisations formed along linguistic and ethnic dimensions to promote the Tamil language and literature as government policy was for national integration and distancing people from their ethnic origins. As the former social organisations declined, there were none to replace them. The community also lacked critical thinkers for providing an intellectual framework to respond to the changing socio-political landscape.

Beginning in the mid-1970s, some tangible directions were observable in the community. From 1975, the newly formed University of Singapore Tamil Language Society set about promoting projects that were to take the community out of its doldrums. The establishment of the society under the guidance of this author (also known as A. Veeramani) and its first conference seminar on Tamil language and Tamil literature in Singapore in 1977 (see Veeramani, 1977), as well its launching of an annual academic bilingual research journal — *Tamil Peravai* — gave new impetus to gathering and examining the direction that Tamil language and literature were taking in Singapore. The biannual 1977, 1979 and 1981 conferences attracted Tamil writers to examine their writing and publications of their works in order to gain the attention of readers and critics. Mere writing or broadcasting was replaced with the need for published evidence to be considered for critical appreciation by others. The conference seminar series was to have a deep impact on crystallising concrete ideas by community leaders to get involved in the community. The next few years witnessed the establishment of the Singapore Association of Tamil Writers in 1977 and the establishment of the Tamil Language and Cultural Society under the patronage of C.V. Devan Nair (1979), a prominent trade unionist and Member of Parliament for Anson constituency. Together with the revival of the Tamils Representative Council (TRC) under another prominent trade unionist, G. Kandasamy, the 1980s appeared to promise hope for the writing and propagation of a Singaporean Tamil literature. Even though the term 'Singapore Tamil literature' came into vogue, publications of Tamil writings were few and far apart. The number of writers remained almost the same and the rate of induction of younger and newer writers was low. One short story writer who tried to buck the trend was Naa Govindasamy, who as a Tamil teacher attempted to set up the *Ilakkia Kalam* (Literary Forum) for adult and student writers and, being an impromptu gathering, it survived for a few years. The TRC Youth Wing under this author's guidance published a number of collections by Singapore-educated Tamil youths, but that too ended in 1987. Most writers did not have the economic sustainability to organise themselves into groups that could induct youths and non-writers to take up serious writing. Tamil literary publications continued with the tireless work of A.P. Shanmugam, who encouraged many writers to publish their writings into books under his *Thai Noolagam* (Thai Publications). In 1989, a gift of S$21,500 raised by fans, friends and readers for a Singapore Tamil poet for his heart operation attracted the attention of Tamil writers in Singapore (*Straits Times*, 15 February 1989, page 14).

The next break for the massive institutional promotion of Tamil literature came in 1990 when Singapore celebrated its 25th anniversary of political independence. Under the auspices of a month-long Indian Cultural Month sponsored by the government, this author again spearheaded a committee backed by the then-dynamic youth movement, the Singapore Tamil Youths Club, to publish 25 books in Tamil and launch them at a single ceremony in April 1990. Twenty-five books were published and launched at a single event, with twenty-three of the books being devoted to Tamil literary writings by young and established writers, both women and men, and consisting of poetry, novels, short stories and dramas. The 1990s witnessed the revival of the Singapore Tamil Writers Association under the leadership of Na. Aandiyappan, who not only promoted events to honour Tamil writers and community stalwarts, but also organised promotional events for Tamil writers' books and organised an International Conference of Tamil Writers in 2011.

Tamil literature underwent rapid changes from the mid-1990s as the new diaspora of Tamil professionals and their spouses in Singapore began to establish their identity in Singapore by involving themselves in literary groups, as well as in publishing Tamil literary collections owing to their closer links to publishers in Tamil Nadu. Government organisations like the National Library and the National Book Development Council began active involvement in the promotion of Tamil literary publications. The exhibitions by the National Library for promoting Tamil literature and the provision of grants for Tamil book publications gave new impetus for the continuing writers and the new diaspora to publish more books in Tamil. It became possible to view all Tamil publications in one place owing to the efforts of the National Library. In the last ten years, the new diaspora of Tamil writers has been honoured in Singapore, Tamil Nadu and elsewhere. The international Tamil diaspora meetings concerning Tamil language also patronised these writers' works.

The contemporary literary scene in Singapore has become highly vibrant with many groups contending for eminence through the publication of their members' books and the promotion of literary events. These include the *Singapoor Thamizh Ilakia Kalam* (Singapore Tamil Literary Forum), the monthly 'story forum' (*Kathai Kalam*) by the Singapore Tamil Writers Association, *Thangameen Vasagar Vattam* (Thangameen Readers Circle), the Singapore Readers Circle (*Singapoor Vasagar Vattam*), *Mathavi Ilakkia Mandram* (Mathavi Literary Society) and *Kavi Maalai* (Poetic Forum). There are leading writers, businessmen and professionals behind these movements, in addition to the many events conducted by individual writers with the patronage of the National Library and the National Book Development Council. These groups coordinate the bestowment of awards by Literary Trusts established in Tamil Nadu by the new diaspora of Tamils. Among the many literary awards is the *Karikala Cholan Award* (named after an ancient Tamil king) given annually at the Thanjavur Tamil University by the Mustapha Foundation. Mohamed Mustapha is a prominent Tamil businessman in Singapore's Little India. Many long-term Tamil writers in Singapore have been honoured by the Cultural Medallion Award by the National Arts Council, the S.E.A. Write Award (Southeast Asian Writers Awards) from Thailand, the Montblanc–NUS Centre for the Arts Literary Award, the Thamizhavel Award from the Association of Singapore Tamil Writers, the Singapore Literature Prize and the Kala Ratna from the Singapore Indian Fine Arts Society (see, for example, Arun Mahizhnan, 2014).

The total production of Tamil literature-related writings in Singapore since 1965 has been estimated as 143 Tamil poetry books, 266 books related to literature for the young, 105 short story books/collections, 48 long and short novels and 176 books based on conference proceedings, essays, critiques, biographies and other Tamil writings (Seetahlakshmi, 2014). Despite the small number of Tamil writers and readers, Tamil literature in Singapore has not only survived, but has become vibrant in the 50 years of Singapore's independence. There is indeed an intense passion among a number of Tamils to become and be a Tamil literati in Singapore.

The impressive production of Tamil literary writings was capped in 2015 by the digitalisation effort of all Tamil literary writings in the years since 1965, to be presented to the Government of Singapore. The digitalisation project and the multi-talented committee was being led by Arun Mahizhnan (*Thamizhmani*, August 2014: 12–13; *Straits Times*, 12 October 2013). Local Tamil heritage groups partnered with the National Library Board in an ambitious plan to digitally record 50 years of Singaporean Tamil creative writing. The 2-year project, begun in 2013, aimed to preserve Tamil literary works for future generations. The project was successfully completed in 2015.

Select References

Arun Mahizhnan, 2014. 'KTM Iqbal: The Man and His Word', *Cultural Medallion 2014*, pp. 18–21. https://nac.gov.sg/docs/awards-recognition-files/ktm-iqbal.pdf. Accessed on 6 February 2015.

Mani A. (2014). A tale of two streets: Urban renewal, transnationalization and reconstructed memories. In: Mani A. (ed) *Enchanting Asian Social Landscapes*. Singapore, Swarnadvipa Publishing House, pp. 1–36.

Seethalakshmi, 2014. *Singapoor Thamizh Ilakkiyam — Oor Arimugam (Singapore Tamil Literature — An Introduction)*. Paper presented at the Conference on *Thayagam Kadantha Thamizh* (Tamil Beyond its Homeland), Coimbatore, Tamil Nadu January 20–22.

Straits Times Newspaper article. Poet receives funds for heart surgery.html. Accessed on 6 February 2015.

Thamizhmani, Quarterly magazine of the Tamil Language and Cultural Society, Singapore, August 2014.

Thinappan SP, Na Aandiyappan, Suba Arunasalam (eds) (2011). *Singapoor Thamizh Ilakia Varalaru — Oor Arimugam (History of Singapore Tamil Literature — An Introduction)*. Singapore, Singapore Tamil Writers Association.

Veeramani A. (1977). *Singapooril Thamizhum Thamizhilakkiyamum (Tamil Language and Tamil Literature in Singapore)*. Singapore, University of Singapore Tamil Language Society.

http://www.straitstimes.com/breaking-news/singapore/story/iswaran-calls-more-volunteers-support-plan-digitise-tamil-literature-2#sthash.rxZVn4Gk.dpuf. Accessed on 3 February 2015.

Mani A., PhD, is Professor at the Ritsumeikan Asia Pacific University, Japan. He was also conferred the title of Professor Emeritus by the University in April 2013. He has worked at the Institute of Southeast Asian Studies (ISEAS), the University of Brunei Darussalam and the National University of Singapore. Currently, he is Visiting Senior fellow at the ISEAS — Yusof Ishak Institute, Singapore. From 1975 to 2000, he developed various programmes and organisations among Indians in Singapore, organised numerous seminars/conferences and published numerous publications in Tamil and English. His wide ranging research includes migration, education and ethnicity in Southeast Asia. Some of his major publications include *Indian Communities in Southeast Asia* (1993), co-edited with K.S. Sandhu; *Campaigning for a Gracious Society in Brunei Darussalam* (1992); *Determinants of Educational Aspirations among Indonesian Youth* (1984); *The Limits of the Nation-State in the Asia Pacific* (2004), edited with Kazuichi Sakamoto; *Rising India and Indians in East Asia* (2008), co-edited with K. Kesavapany and P. Ramasamy; *Early Interactions between South Asia and Southeast Asia: Reflections on Cross-Cultural Exchange* (2011), co-edited with P.Y. Manguin and Geoff Wade; and *Enchanting Asian Social Landscapes* (2014). Currently, he is researching on *Sufism in South India and Southeast Asia*; the *Impact of South Indian Reform Movements on Tamils in Southeast Asia*; *Displacement and Responses among Tamils in the Greater Klang Valley Region*; and *Interethnic Interactions in Yangon, Myanmar*.

7 'Rising from the Ashes': The Development of Hindi in Independent Singapore

Rajesh Rai

Hindi has always had a tentative position in Singapore's multicultural setting. In the public sphere, initially Malay, and now English, serves as the lingua franca for inter-ethnic communication.[1] Even in the Indian community in Singapore, Hindi speakers comprise a 'minority within a minority' — a corollary of large-scale immigration from southern India historically, which ensured that Tamil speakers constituted the largest component of the Indian population here. Consequently, for much of Singapore's history, interaction in Hindi tended to be confined to "the domains of the home, for interaction with relatives ... [co-ethnic] friends, and for community related uses."[2] That said, over the last 25 years, Hindi has emerged as the fastest-growing Indian language in Singapore, and its visibility in the public sphere now extends well beyond just the Hindi-speaking community. This chapter historicises the changing position of the Hindi language in Singapore, with a focus on developments after independence in 1965. In so doing, the chapter examines the historical development of the language in Singapore to provide context; it explains how specific policies adopted by the state after 1965 resulted in the near attrition of the language in the city by the late 1980s; and goes on to analyse why the language has, metaphorically, 'risen from the ashes' to its current position of strength.

---

[1] Afendras EA., Kuo ECY. (eds) (1980) *Language and Society in Singapore*. Singapore, Singapore University Press, p. 48.
[2] Singh SA. (1994). *A Sociolinguistic Study of Diminished Proficiency in Hindi within Two Hindi Households*. Academic Exercise (unpublished), NUS, p. 2.

Historical Background

The arrival of Hindi speakers, or more precisely speakers of Hindi's 'sister' languages — Hindustani and Bhojpuri — can be dated to the British 'founding' of the settlement in 1819. The earliest Indian troops deployed by the East India Company (EIC) in Singapore hailed from the Hindustani/Bhojpuri-speaking regions of eastern Uttar Pradesh and north-western Bihar.[3] Early observer accounts suggest that when Singapore was administered as a part of British India (until 1867), British officials and merchants — who received Hindustani language education — as well as Armenian Christian, Baghdadi Jew and Parsi traders who arrived from India used the language when communicating with their Indian subordinates in Singapore. A Hindustani interpreter was employed by the Singapore Courts, and the language was the lingua franca of the large penal settlement for transported Indian convicts in Singapore from 1825 to 1873.[4]

The use of Hindustani in the British administration in Singapore declined following the separation of the Straits Settlements from British India in 1867. In the late 19th century, the language was spoken mainly by the small number of migrants from what is today referred to as the 'Hindi heartland' in India. Those from Gujarat, Punjab, Sind and Bengal were also conversant in Hindustani, which was used for communicating with others from northern parts of India. Notwithstanding the small community of native speakers, Hindustani performances had a distinct presence in Singapore's budding cultural scene in the late 19th and early 20th centuries. From the 1880s, theatrical groups such as the Parsee Victoria Theatrical Company, the Parsee Opera and the Indra Zanzibar Theatrical Company organised regular dramatic performances in Hindustani (sometimes combined with a sprinkling English and Malay) at the Parsee Theatre by the Raffles Hotel, and later at 'Happy Valley' and 'New World'. Their productions, such as 'Alladin and the Forty Thieves' and the epic Indian love story 'Laily and Mujnoon', drew a multi-ethnic mix of high society in Singapore, including Europeans who had only a delicate hold of the language.[5] The advent of Hindi cinema in the early 20th century also had an immediate impact on the city's dwellers — a dramatic rendition of 'Raja Harishchandra' in 1915 by the Young Men's Arya Samaj in Singapore was inspired by the release of the Dadasaheb Phalke's first full-length Hindi inter-titled film bearing the same name.[6]

---

[3] See Rai R. (2004). Sepoys, convicts and the "bazaar" contingent: The emergence and the exclusion of "Hindustani" pioneers at the Singapore frontier. Journal of Southeast Asian Studies, **35**(1): pp. 1–19.

[4] Rai R. (2014). Indians in Singapore, 1819–1945: Diaspora in the Colonial Port City. New Delhi, Oxford University Press, p. 15.

[5] The Straits Times, various issues from the 1880s to the 1920s.

[6] The Straits Times, 21 May 1916, p. 6.

Several factors informed the early development of formal Hindi language education in Singapore in the inter-war period. Some were intrinsic. Elders in the Hindi-speaking community in Singapore were concerned that the younger generation could not read or write the language and so initially turned to tutors to educate their children. Developments in India also influenced Indians here to learn the language. The spread of nationalist politics there resulted in fractiousness between advocates of Hindi and Urdu, with the Indian Congress favouring Hindi, or the more syncretic Hindustani, as the national language for independent India in the future. Records suggest that the Arya Samaj was probably the first institution in Singapore to hold regular Hindi classes from 1930, and this was later continued under the auspices of its educational affiliate, the Dayanand Anglo Vedic (DAV) School.[7] By the late 1930s, especially after the Indian Congress's (INC) victory in the 1936–7 Indian provincial elections, Hindi was also taken up by upper-middle-class and middle-class Indians from non-Hindi-speaking homes. For example, Vilasini Perumbulavil — from a Malayalam-speaking family — took Hindi tuition in the 1930s because her father felt that "being Indian, we ought to learn [Hindi]."[8] Prior to the advent of the Second World War, Hindi classes were also being organised at the Naval Base area and at the premises of the Indian Youth League at Race Course Road.[9]

During the Japanese occupation, Hindi gained ascendancy in the Indian population. Under the Mohan Singh-led Indian National Army (INA), Hindi was utilised as the language of command in the army and for administrative purposes at the Indian Independence League (IIL) and for its publications, and Indian children were encouraged to learn the language. At the time, the offices of the local Tamil Reforms Association (TRA), which had previously condemned Congress's advocacy of Hindi as the future national language of India, were also shut down. Under Rash Behari Bose's leadership of the Indian National Movement in East Asia (until June 1943), attendance at Hindi schools in Singapore increased and the youth militia of the INA — the *Balak Sena* and the *Balika Sena* — were required to learn Hindi. When Subhas Chandra Bose took over leadership of the INA (July 1943–August 1945), the more syncretic Hindustani — with a blend of Hindi and Urdu — was emphasised, partly to win over Indian Muslim support for the movement.[10]

---

[7] *The Singapore Free Press*, 27 January 1931, p. 18; *The Singapore Free Press*, 22 January 1934, p. 3.
[8] National Archives of Singapore (NAS), Oral History Interview Accession No.: 002437, Reel No.: 3, Interviewee: Perumbulavil Vilasini, 28 September 2000.
[9] NAS, Oral History Interview Accession No.: 000025, Reel No.: 1, Interviewee: Dr. K.R. Menon, 26 February 1982.
[10] Rai R. (2014). *Indians in Singapore, 1819–1945: Diaspora in the colonial port city*. New Delhi, Oxford University Press, pp. 247–248.

Advocates of the Hindi language faced serious challenges after the Second World War. Although newly independent India recognised Hindi in the Devanagri script as the official language of the Indian Union, the language received no support from the British administration in Singapore. Instead, the rejuvenated TRA, now known as the Tamils Representative Council (TRC), was able to press British support for Tamil vernacular education. Consequently, it was left to the small Hindi-speaking community to sustain Hindi education in Singapore, which in the post-War period and the 1950s was run at the Netaji Hindi High School and the DAV School.[11] The implementation of stricter migration controls in the 1950s added to these difficulties. To the extent that new arrivals from the 'homeland' had a regenerative influence on the language, these migration controls resulted in the diasporic community being increasingly isolated from the 'homeland'.

Hindi in Independent Singapore

When Singapore gained independence in 1965, the constitution recognised four official languages — English and three languages representing each of the main 'races' in Singapore (i.e. Mandarin for the Chinese, Malay for the Malays and Tamil for Indians). The inclusion of Tamil and the exclusion of Hindi as the official language representing Indians was the outcome of specific demographic and political factors. Tamil speakers constituted the overwhelming majority of the Indian population in Singapore at the time of independence. Moreover, the politicisation of labour preceding Singapore's independence had also seen stewardship of the Indian community pass into the hands of those associated with Tamil labour and who were exposed to Tamil vernacular education. This "effectively placed community education in the hands of Tamil school masters [who were] fascinated by the Dravidian movement in India."[12] The popularity of that movement amongst Tamils, with its pro-Tamil and anti-Hindi agenda, also influenced the decision to reject Hindi as the representative language for Indians in Singapore.

The exclusion of Hindi as an official language had repercussions in language education. The bilingual policy, which was adopted in the national curriculum in 1966, required the study of two languages. English was advocated for due to economic reasons, along with one other official language to provide a 'cultural ballast' for the different races. However, the notion that the language representing the

---

[11] Rai R. (2009). The attrition and survival of minor South Asian languages in Singapore. In: Rai R., Reeves P. (eds) *The South Asian Diaspora: Transnational Networks and Changing Identities*. London, Routledge, p. 149.

[12] Rai R. (2004). 'Race' and the construction of the North–South divide amongst Indians in colonial Malaya and Singapore. *Journal of South Asian Studies* **27**(2): p. 258.

racial group necessarily provided a 'cultural ballast' was questionable. Most Hindi speakers could not understand, speak or write Tamil. Worse still, the bilingual policy imposed a strain on children from these Hindi-speaking homes, who were now required to learn two foreign languages. This in turn affected interest in learning their 'mother tongue'. Glenda Michelle Singh informs us that:

> ... right up to 1965, Indian students were permitted to offer Hindi at 'O' and 'A' level ... After Independence in 1965 ... Hindi could not be offered as a subject in schools. Consequently, interest in studying it declined.[13]

To reduce their distress, the state permitted Indian students whose 'mother tongue' was not Tamil to study any of the three second languages on offer. Although students from Hindi-speaking homes could take up Malay — considered to be "easier to pick up than Tamil or Mandarin"[14] and useful for inter-ethnic communication — or Mandarin — considered economically more useful than either Tamil or Malay — the policy did not address concerns that the national curriculum did not provide an avenue for these children to learn their own 'mother tongue'. Consequently, from the 1960s to the 1980s, children from Hindi-speaking homes could only learn their 'mother tongue' through community-run schools. But there was little motivation to study Hindi given the negligible value of learning their 'mother tongue' for educational and career advancement and the limited communicative domains for the language in Singapore. The only reason for youngsters to learn Hindi was emotional, to converse with monolingual elders in the Hindi-speaking community or for entertainment (i.e. to understand Hindi movies). Most youngsters could sustain such a level of understanding in the 'mother tongue' without attending formal classes. Consequently, community-based language institutions saw declining numbers. As early as the 1970s, the Netaji Hindi High School closed due to a lack of interest and support.[15] While the DAV Hindi School persevered, students attending its Hindi class in the 1970s usually numbered less than 40, and attrition rates were high. Classes were run only once a week with a mix of children and adults from the Hindi-speaking community and adults from the Malay community (who had an interest in the language because of the popularity of Hindi cinema). By the

---

[13] Singh GM (1994). *Sociolinguistic Influences on the Maintenance of Hindi in Singapore*. M.A. Thesis (unpublished), NUS, p. 21.

[14] Ramakanthan R. (1989). *The Organized Management of the Tamil Language in Singapore: A Kaleidoscopic Description of the Different Aspects and the Problems Involved*. M.A. Thesis (unpublished), NUS, p. 43.

[15] Rai R. (2009). The attrition and survival of minor South Asian languages in Singapore. In: Rai R, Reeves P. (eds) *The South Asian Diaspora: Transnational Networks and Changing Identities*. London, Routledge, p. 149.

1980s, Hindi language proficiency in the Hindi-speaking community had depreciated considerably. While statistics specific to Hindi are not available, Gopinathan posits that the percentage of Indians literate in 'other' (non-Tamil) Indian languages declined from 5.2% in 1970 to 1.7% in 1980.[16] The Hindi language effectively stood at the brink of 'death' in Singapore by the mid-1980s. Indeed, besides Hindi-speaking homes, the only domains where Hindi was spoken were the few institutions run by northern Indians, such as the Arya Samaj and the DAV School, the North Indian Hindu Association and the Shri Lakshminarayan Temple.

Remarkable Turnaround

The 1990s saw a remarkable turnaround in the position of the Hindi language in Singapore. The relaxation of migration controls for educated personnel provided a lifeline. Seen as necessary to maintain and renew Singapore's competitive edge following growing out-migration of talented Singaporeans and as an antidote to concerns of an ageing population, the migration of 'foreign talent' was encouraged from the late 1980s. Chinese and Indian professionals were preferred due to the perception that they could easily assimilate with co-ethnic counterparts in Singapore. Consequently, a new group of first-generation Indian migrant professionals emerged. These migrants were, ethno-linguistically, more heterogeneous than the erstwhile Indian diaspora in Singapore, and many were literate in Hindi.

Even more than the migration of professionals, the position of Hindi strengthened because sustained lobbying by the non-Tamil-speaking Indian communities for the inclusion of their 'mother tongue' in the educational curriculum succeeded. Their arguments were twofold: a) that studying their 'mother tongue' would enable children from these communities to understand their culture better; and b) that non-Tamil 'Indian' students were having difficulty in coping with Tamil, Chinese or Malay as a second language.[17] It was the latter argument that proved decisive. A high-level task force investigating Indian underachievement in education confirmed the following:

> The second language grades obtained by non-Tamil Indian students, who are unable to take their mother tongue for the purpose, have weakened their overall performance in primary school examinations. The

---

[16]Gopinathan S. Language policy change 1979–1997: Politics and pedagogy. In: Gopinathan S., Pakir A., Kam HW., Saravanan V. (eds) *Language, Society and Education in Singapore: Issues and Trends*, p. 37.

[17]Jin CC. (1990). Encouraging number of pupils take minority Indian languages as L2. *Straits Times*, 2 February 1990, p. 24.

Indian pass rate in second language at 'O' levels, at 85% in 1990, also falls short of the Chinese pass rate of 94%. This is despite the Indian pass rate in Tamil (TL2) being on par with Chinese students' performance, and reflects the special weakness of non-Tamil Indian students in the second language.[18]

In 1990, the Ministry of Education, as part of wider reforms in second language study, recognised five non-Tamil Indian languages (i.e. Hindi, Punjabi, Bengali, Urdu and Gujarati) at 'O' level, and extended recognition for these subjects in 1991, at 'AO' levels in 1992 and at 'N' level and at PSLE level in 1994. However, unlike Singapore's official languages, the government provided limited support for education in these languages (i.e. school premises could be used for lessons, but provision for education in these languages would be dependent on financial support and the initiative of the respective communities). Moreover, unlike the four official languages, government campaigns and official media would neither use nor promote these languages.

Since this momentous decision, the number of students learning Hindi in Singapore has risen dramatically. Prior to recognition in the curriculum, less than 50 students were studying the language. By 2000, the number crossed to over 3000 students, and in 2015, the number taking Hindi as part of the national curriculum exceeded 6500 (from K1 to 'A' levels). This figure does not include students learning Hindi at International Schools. Indeed, the number of students taking Hindi is now more than double the combined total of all the other non-Tamil Indian language (i.e. Punjabi, Bengali, Urdu and Gujarati) students in Singapore schools. Hindi language is also offered at the tertiary level, and since its introduction, it has drawn more students than any other Indian language offered by the Centre of Language Studies at the National University of Singapore.

Several factors account for the sharp increase in the number of students learning Hindi. This is not just because of migrant professionals from the 'Hindi heartland', who comprise a minority of those emigrating from India, but rather due to the dominant position of Hindi in India. This has resulted in a diverse group — not constrained to those who originate from Hindi-speaking regions in India — encouraging their children to learn the language. While it may be that their children have taken up Hindi because their 'mother tongue' is not available in the curriculum (e.g. Marathi, Sindhi, Kannada, Malayalee, Telugu, etc.), the turn to Hindi is also reflective of their incipient position in Singapore. Since many new migrants view Singapore as a temporary stop, and may consider returning to India,

---

[18]Singapore Action Committee on Indian Education (1991). *At the Crossroads: Report of the Action Committee on Indian Education*. Singapore, p. 11.

their choice of language is influenced by the position of Hindi in India, where as the federal union official language, it is compulsory to learn Hindi in primary school.[19] Consequently, even when the option of learning their 'mother tongue' is available (i.e. Tamil, Punjabi, Gujarati, Bengali and Urdu), many have chosen to learn Hindi as a second language.

Beyond changes in the curriculum, the position of Hindi in Singapore has been buttressed by the popularity of transnational Hindi media. The number of cinemas screening Hindi films has increased, a return to strength after the decline in the 1980s when the advent of video cassette recorders led to the closure of several halls. Their success is intrinsically connected to the tremendous growth of the Indian immigrant population, for whom watching a Hindi movie at the cinema remains a cherished social activity. A Hindi-speaking informant captures the current popularity of Hindi cinema-going in Singapore through a personal anecdote:

> In September 2009, my wife and I decided to watch a Hindi movie at Jade Cineplex. As we nuzzled through the crowd of Indian migrant professionals to buy our tickets, we found that not only was the screening at 8pm fully booked, so was the next show at 11.45. Desperately we tried to locate another cinema hall that was screening that movie and discovered that many others cinema that traditionally never showed [sic.] Hindi movies were screening [the movie]. We managed to get tickets for the midnight show at another Cineplex, but even that show was packed so that by that time of our arrival, we were left only with front row seats. After another such incident, we have reconciled to paying extra for advance tickets.[20]

The advent of cable TV in Singapore has added another layer of Hindi entertainment available in Singapore. Whereas Hindi-speakers from the 1960s to the 1980s could only watch the once-weekly Hindi movie on the national channel dedicated to Indians, viewers can now subscribe to more than 10 Hindi channels via cable TV. A Hindi radio station, *Masti 96.3 FM*, has, since 2007, been airing at a 3-hour primetime slot on Singapore's dedicated international language radio channel. In the popular culture scene, Singapore has, since the 2000s, been a choice location for Hindi cinema award ceremonies and other Hindi cultural productions, including dramatic performances and musicals, which nearly always draw packed audiences. Hindi songs are now common fayre in top discotheques. Several estates on the eastern coastline of Singapore now have large Hindi-speaking populations,

---

[19] Sonntag SK. (2002). Minority language politics in North India. In: Tollefson JW. (ed) *Language Policies in Education: Critical Issues*. London, LEA Publishers, p. 166.

[20] Author's interview with a lawyer who has chosen to remain anonymous, 13 April 2015.

and these have become domains where the language is heavily utilised. A similar scenario is evident in certain knowledge-based industries, such as the information technology sector. Possibly the most telling reflection of the position of Hindi in contemporary Singapore is the fact that even in shared public spaces — be it at hawker centres, shopping malls, playgrounds or schools — finding Indians conversing in Hindi is no longer cause for surprise.

Conclusion

The position of Hindi in Singapore has witnessed tremendous changes over the last 50 years. State policies and imperatives are the causes of these changes. The introduction, soon after independence, of the bilingual policy in education focused only on the four official languages, resulted in the near attrition of Hindi in the public domain. Indeed, by the 1980s, few of the younger generation from Hindi-speaking homes were literate in their mother tongue. The turnaround in Hindi's position since the 1990s is likewise the outcome of changes in state policy vis-à-vis language education. The recognition that the second language policies in education that limited choice to the four official languages had a detrimental impact on student performance in minority Indian communities led to the inclusion of Hindi (and four other Indian languages) in the curriculum. This resulted in a rapid increase in the number of students learning Hindi, far exceeding that of any other non-Tamil Indian language. In addition, the migration of professionals from India since the 1990s has also had an important impact on the position of Hindi. Beyond providing 'regenerative' contact, the flexibility available to Indians in choosing their 'mother tongue' has resulted in Hindi drawing students from beyond its immediate target community, particularly since concerns of return weigh heavily on the minds of these new migrants. While new Hindi domains have emerged due to new migrant professionals arriving from India, its position is also vulnerable for the very same reason. Although student numbers taking the language have shown a persistent increase over the last 25 years, many new migrants have also exercised the option of 'return' to India, or re-migrated to the US, UK, Australia, Canada or New Zealand. The future prospects of the language in Singapore therefore remain closely tied to in-migration. Consequently, an increase or decline in economic opportunities in India, Singapore or possible re-migration locations, or a change in government policy towards more stringent migrant controls, are all variables that could have significant impacts on the position of Hindi. But for now, the language is better placed than ever before in the history of independent Singapore.

Rajesh Rai is Deputy Head and Associate Professor at the South Asian Studies Programme, National University of Singapore. His research interests are in the area of diaspora studies, nationalism and the postcolonial history and politics of South Asia. Author of *Indians in Singapore, 1819–1945: Diaspora in the Colonial Port City* (Oxford University Press, 2014), he has also edited several major works on the South Asian diaspora including *The Encyclopedia of the Sri Lankan Diaspora* (with Peter Reeves and Hema Kiruppalini, 2013); *Religion and Identity in the South Asian Diaspora* (with Chitra Sankaran, 2013); *South Asian Diaspora: Transnational Networks and Changing Identities* (with Peter Reeves, 2009); and *The Encyclopedia of the Indian Diaspora* (with Brij Lal and Peter Reeves, 2006). Rai's articles have been published in premier academic journals such as *Modern Asian Studies, South Asia: Journal of South Asian Studies*, *Journal of Southeast Asian Studies* and *South Asian Diaspora*. He has a passion for teaching and has received several teaching awards at NUS. When he manages some "free time," he enjoys playing chess.

8 Indian Writing in English

Meira Chand

The majority of the resident Indian community in Singapore is of South Indian origin, particularly of Tamil ancestry. Early settlers, many of whom were indentured labourers, brought with them to Singapore their traditions, languages and a strong sense of culture. In Singapore, Indian writers, using both English and in the vernacular, have developed the genres of poetry, drama and the short story to particular relevance, and these literary forms still remain more popular than the genre of the novel. Yet, the pool of Indian writing in English as compared to the body of writing in the vernacular is small. A portion of Tamil writing is translated into English, but few Tamil writers write directly in the English language, and translations are not considered in this short assessment.

Early writers and poets of the Diaspora, like all early Diasporic writers anywhere, looked homewards and wrote from a sense of exile, often drawing strongly on the myths and legends of the past. Of special influence in the Indian culture was the tradition of oral storytelling, rooted in the epic narratives of the *Mahabharata* and the *Ramayana*. Indian poets and writers in today's Singapore who write in the vernacular easily draw on this rich heritage as they examine the tensions that come from a traditional community facing the multicultural influences of a modern Singapore and the gradual loss of language and old customs. These writers often seem to retain a stronger sense of connection to India in their work than Singaporean Indians writing in English, where issues of identity appear to be more problematic.

The problems faced by Indian writers in English are complex. Although the Singaporean poets Edwin Thumboo and Chandran Nair do draw on their heritage and make reference in some of their works to the ancient myths and legends of Hinduism, in general, a multiplicity of other cultural themes dominates their writing. However, in a recent interview Edwin Thumboo states how his Indian heritage gave him "a sense of tradition provided by our ancestral histories, a need for a hinterland that goes beyond our little red dot into the earlier history of Southeast Asia with its strong Indian underpinning" (Thumboo 2014).

Until independence, English education in Singapore was a colonial enterprise, the history studied was British and the worlds examined were imported and alien. The link between language and literature is deeply organic; they are the vehicles upon which culture is encoded. As such, a special layer of tension confronts Indian writers and poets writing in the English language. As the global lingua franca, English has been essential to the modernisation of Singapore, yet it carries with it Western conventions and ideals, and transmits values alien to traditional Indian points of reference. Indian writing in English in Singapore is influenced more by the legacy of this history of colonialism, with its English education, than by Indian heritage. However, according to the poet and academic Kirpal Singh, for Indian writers, "it is in the values and attitudes contained in their writing that their Indianness manifests itself" (Singh 1992). In this way, Indian writers who write in English are forced to negotiate between multiple worlds, including religion and language, forever treading a road between the colonial past and a modern independent reality.

Indian writers in Singapore, who use the English language write as Singaporeans, examining their sense of self, their connection to the local world around them and their engagement with Singapore and Singaporean issues. While in many other countries writers of different ethnicities form distinct sub-groups (e.g. Indian writers in America, Chinese writers in Canada, etc.), writers of Indian ethnicity in Singapore are seen only as Singaporean writers. Perhaps it can be said that these writers have made the transition from exile to native. Diaspora no longer concerns them to any great degree. Edwin Thumboo says that, "the freedom from Exile is a release from having an alternative to whom and where you are. It is the prelude to relocating culture with which comes greater management of image, metaphor and symbol as they acquire a local habitation" (Thumboo 1988). Singaporean Indians writing in English would appear to have made the long transitional journey through difficult post-colonial terrain, to the wholeness of a new and unique Singaporean identity.

As previously stated, the number of Singaporean Indians writing in English is small, although many young writers are now emerging. Whether these new writers will continue to grow to a point where they can be added to the core group remains to be seen. For now, the best known of the group are Edwin Thumboo, Gopal Barathnam, Chandran Nair, Philip Jayaratnam, Kirpal Singh and Barish Sharma. They are a multiracial group with several having a non-Indian parent or spouse, thus expanding their roots to other ethnic communities.

Edwin Thumboo is often called Singapore's unofficial Poet Laureate. More than any other writer in English, Thumboo has established the way for all those who came after him. He was one of the earliest poets to publish his work, believing that post-independence poets and writers were responsible for creating a national literature. His poetry spans more than 50 years and chronicles and celebrates the making of modern Singapore. His twin Indian and Chinese heritages give him an ideal vantage point from which to examine the political, social and cultural aspects of life in the developing nation state.

In an introduction to *The Best of Edwin Thumboo* (2012), Lily Rose Trope notes that he "connects poet and country to global culture and creates a cartography of a poet, citizen and man." Thumboo's political and social consciousness underlies much of his work and is nowhere more apparent than in works such as *Rib of Earth* (1956), *Gods Can Die* (1977) and *Ulysses by the Merlion* (1979).

Chandran Nair's poetry has received great critical acclaim, both locally and internationally. Although born in Kerela, India, he came to Singapore at the age of seven and began writing early. His two collections of poetry, *Once the Horseman and Other Poems* (1972) and *After the Hard Hours This Rain* (1975), incorporate an exceptionally Indian sensibility with references to Indian myths, legends, landscape and spirituality. Edwin Thumboo commends Nair for this ability to weave East and West into an inter-textuality of language and metaphor.

Kirpal Singh was born in Singapore to a Sikh father and British mother. A poet and academic, he has written two collections of poetry, *Psalm Readings* (1986) and *Cat Walking and the Games We Play* (1998), as well as numerous academic and critical essays and edited many prestigious journals. He is known more for his research and writings in the areas of post-colonial literature, Singapore and South East Asian literature and creative thinking, which he teaches at Singapore Management University.

Philip Jayaratnam is the author of several award-winning novels and short story collections that examine life and the social attitudes of modern Singapore. The son of prominent opposition activist lawyer, J.B. Jayaratnam, and an English mother who was also a lawyer, Jayaratnam has continued the family tradition and is a Senior Counsel. His book *First Loves* (1987), a collection of linked shmi stories, was a Singapore bestseller, and his novel *Raffles Place Ragtime* (1988) was nominated for the Commonwealth Writers Prize. *Abraham's Promise* (1994) was his second novel. Amongst other awards, he has won the Airey Neave Award and the South Asia Write Award.

Gopal Baratham was a neurosurgeon and is an author of both controversial fiction and non-fiction. Baratham's work was deeply influence by his personal experiences. Growing up during the years of World War II, he knew well the effects of colonialism and racism and drew on his experiences in his work, as well as the themes of industrialisation and modernisation he had seen during a life lived through the seminal events of modern Singapore's history. He was awarded the S.E.A. (South-East Asia) Write Award in 1991 for his collection of short stories, *People Make You Cry and Other Stories,* and his novel, *A Candle or the Sun,* was shortlisted for Best Book in the 1992 Commonwealth Writers' Prize.

Harish Sharma is known primarily as a poet and playwright. He won the Singapore Literature Prize in 1993 for his play, *Still Building,* and received the Young Artist Award from the National Arts Council. He is Resident Playwright of The Necessary Stage. His play, *Of! Centre,* was the first Singaporean play to become an O-level literature text. Much of Sharma's work draws on themes of Singaporean relevance and social issues, such as mental illness, inter-racial relations, AIDS and the educational system in Singapore.

These core Indian Singaporean writers, and those younger writers that are now emerging, see themselves and their work not in the context of their Indian roots, but in the larger context of a national Singaporean identity that is formed not by looking inwards and backwards, but by defining themselves in relation to the modern life around them.

Dr. Meire Chand of Indian-Swiss heritage, was born and educated in London. She has lived extensively in Japan and in India, but now resides in Singapore and is a Singaporean citizen. Her multicultural heritage is reflected in her eight novels that explore issues of identity and belonging. In the UK, her latest novel, *A Different Sky* was a book-of-the-month choice by the bookshop chain Waterstones, long listed for the IMPAC Dublin literary award, and on Oprah Winfrey's reading list. She has a PhD in Creative Writing and is involved in programmes in Singapore to nurture and promote young writers.

Indian Political Participation in Singapore

Asad Latif

Indian political participation in Singapore goes far back into the city's colonial history. However, it was cast in sharp relief following Japan's defeat in World War II. Although the Indian National Army (INA) had failed to liberate India with Japan's help, the struggle for India's independence unleashed a burst of insurgent energy among Indians in Singapore and Malaya. That radicalism proved to be resilient when it planted its roots in local soil. Singapore Indians turned their attention away from their role in India's independence to the anti-colonial struggle against the British returning to their own region.

Indians focused on immediate, material issues, such as labour. Former INA personnel led the effort to form the Indian sections of the General Labour Unions in Malaya. A working-class alliance between Indians and Chinese emerged in 1946 from collaboration between former INA members and their nationalist counterparts in the Malayan Communist Party. There also were independent unions set up by partisans of the INA and the Indian Independence League, for example, the Perak Indian Labour Association headed by M.C.P. Menon.[1]

A tentative multi-racialism of the free, emerging from an exhilarating sense of inhabiting political territory in the making that was not foreclosed by colonialism, race or religion, allowed Indians to seek their place in these new times. The desired homeland of emancipation was no longer India but Singapore and Malaya. The terrain was economic, and the politics were local.

One strain of activity involved 'high politics'. Indians were active in the constitutional politics of the late-colonial period, acting as early spokesmen for popular aspirations for self-rule that even the British knew could not be contained or co-opted forever. Nazir Ahmad Mallal and Mohamed Javad Namazie embodied

---

[1]Sengupta N. (2012). *A Gentleman's Word: The Legacy of Subhas Chanda Bose in Southeast Asia*. Singapore, Institute of Southeast Asian Studies, p. 179.

the Indian political imprint left on the period. One of three leaders of the Singapore Progressive Party (PP), the first political party to contest elections, N.A. Mallal was elected to the First Legislative Council in 1948; M.J. Namazie was elected to the Council as an independent candidate. Other names identified with elite politics are those of Arumugam Ponnu Rajah, the PP's first secretary who was elected a city councillor in 1949, and Legislative Councillors C.R. Dasaratha Raj and S.C. Goho.

Simultaneously, however, there was another, grassroots strain. The turn to the Fabian left that was registered during those years was inscribed in the Singapore Labour Party's inauguration in 1948, with which the unionist M.P.D. Nair is associated intimately. Unionist S. Jaganathan, leader of the Singapore Trades Union Congress in the 1950s, is another example of the community's contribution to the labour movement, which provided a vital overlap between the economic life and the political destiny of a nascent Singapore.

On the party political front, Indian participation played an integral role in sustaining the momentum for Singapore's self-governance during the transitional era of the David Marshall and Lim Yew Hock governments. The businessman Rajabali Jumabhoy was appointed to the Executive Council of the Legislative Assembly in 1951 and elected to the Legislative Council as an Independent in the first general election in 1955. His son, J.M. Jumabhoy, was Minister for Commerce and Industry from 1956 to 1959.

The patrician politics of the period were shaken to their core by the advent of the People's Action Party (PAP) in 1954. The presence of the former jailed communist, Chengara Veetil Devan Nair, at the party's inauguration heralded the role of Indians in the transformative making of a democratic socialist Singapore. His strong roots in the labour movement propelled him to the highest ranks of the National Trades Union Congress, and ultimately to the presidency. Indeed, the PAP's success in marginalising communist-dominated trade unions owes much to the organisational, theoretical and communicative skills that Devan Nair had brought with him from his communist years, along with his unquestionable integrity and commitment to the welfare of the people. Another Indian stalwart, the civil servant and diplomat Sellapan Ramanathan, also had intimate experience of dealing with labour issues among the many portfolios in which he had distinguished himself. As Elected President, he remained a man of the people — not just Indians, but Singaporeans generally — who was equally comfortable shaking the hands of workers and statesmen like himself. These two Indian Singaporean icons worked in a multiracial environment moulded by Cabinet Minister Sinnathamby Rajaratnam, one of the core members of the PAP's old guard. It is difficult to imagine today's Singapore without his deep and abiding commitment to multiracialism, which went hand in hand with other ideals enshrined in the National Pledge, which he wrote.

Succeeding generations of Cabinet leaders drawn from the Indian community continued to advance Indian interests, not as parochial politicians, but as nationalists who understood that minority interests could be safeguarded only with the comfort and concurrence of the majority. In this, they contributed to the ethos of Singapore's multiracial political system, where leaders of every community use the national credibility they gain to articulate sectional interests (whether ethnic or occupational). This is unlike leadership in systems based on ethnic alliances, where community leaders seek to achieve national stature on the basis of their credibility in their particular communities. The introduction of Group Representation Constituencies in the 1980s ensured minority representation in Parliament, indicating to Indians that their ethnic interests would not be sacrificed at the altar of political expediency.

Many illustrious Indians have contributed to the community's political representation by working within a multiracial framework that seeks to balance national and ethnic interests. At the Cabinet level, they are Suppiah Dhanabalan, Shunmugam Jayakumar, Tharman Shanmugaratnam, Kasiviswanathan Shanmugam, Vivian Balakrishnan, S. Iswaran and Balaji Sadasivan. They are joined by a long list of other Indian parliamentarians in the PAP. Since the 1980s, they have included S. Chandra Das, Sushilan Vasoo, Davinder Singh, R. Sinnakaruppan, Ramasamy Ravindran, Inderjit Singh, Indranee Rajah, Hri Kumar, Vikram Nair and Daryl David. Several Indians made their mark as Nominated Members of Parliament, while on the opposition slate, Joshua Benjamin Jeyaretnam carved out a highly visible role both inside and outside of Parliament.

The story of Indians' political participation is set to continue in terms of both its depth and its intensity.

Asad Latif came from India to Singapore in 1984 to work as a journalist, first for *The Business Times* and then for *The Straits Times*. He took his Honours in English at Presidency College, Kolkata, and read History at Clare Hall, Cambridge, where he was a Chevening (Raffles) and an S. Rajaratnam Scholar. He was a Jefferson Fellow at the East-West Center and a Fulbright Visiting Scholar at Harvard.

Asad Latif is the author of *India in the Making of Singapore*.

10 The Indian Contribution to Singapore's Economic Development

Manu Bhaskaran

At around 9% of the population, a share that has not changed hugely over the last 100 years, the Indian community has contributed a reasonable share of the labour force, professional class and business community of Singapore for a long time. This article traces the evolution of Indians as an economic influence in Singapore over the years.

The Indian Contribution Started Very Early and has Expanded Since

Well before the re-founding of Singapore by Stamford Raffles in 1819, Indian merchants and traders were known to have frequented the trading hubs that had operated in and around Singapore through the 700 years of Singapore's extended history — although there is little in the historic record that gives us much in the way of details. The one good record we have of the earliest recorded Indian arrivals in the Singapore vicinity was King Rajendra Chola's invasion in 1025, which destroyed a thriving trading hub at the tip of the Malay Peninsula — but that 'contribution' is perhaps best forgotten!

We have more information on the substantial role Indians played in the economic development of modern Singapore from 1819 onwards, and that is what this article will focus on. In essence, Indians contributed in many ways and from an early stage, through multiple waves of migration that brought in traders, labourers and professionals. The children of those who stayed went on to become business and community leaders, while some of them rose to prominent roles in economic policy.

Indeed, the Indian contribution started almost immediately from the moment Raffles and his deputy William Farquhar landed in Singapore in 1819. Both men were accompanied by Narayana Pillai, an Indian trader who had been based in Penang. He was the first construction contractor in Singapore and is known to have started the first brick kiln in Tanjong Pagar. Pillai also diversified into the retail sector, establishing a successful bazaar selling cotton goods. He not only contributed to the early economic growth of Singapore, but also to the social and cultural development of the Indian community. For example, he helped to build the Sri Mariamman Temple in 1828, which still stands today as Singapore's oldest Hindu temple.

Strong Contribution in Business, Professional Services and Construction

The Indian contribution to economic development varied over time, with the different waves of immigration bringing diverse groups of Indians to the island. One group contributed to the construction of early Singapore. In the early colonial period, starting from the 1820s, the colonial authorities found it convenient to bring in large numbers of Indians to help them build infrastructure, as well as to administer the growing city and its vital port and trading centre. Indian labour was recruited by the Straits Settlements government to undertake public and construction works. As the 19th century progressed, Singapore's trading hub prospered and its population increased, necessitating the building of even more infrastructure. These later developments — road construction, railways, bridges and major buildings — were carried out by convicts from India who were involved in hard labour. Prominent structures built by these labourers include St. Andrews Cathedral, Government House (now City Hall) and the Causeway to Johor.

A second group of Indians that the colonial government relied on were the mainly English-educated South Indians, Ceylon Tamils and Sikhs that came in to help the colonial authorities administer the city. This latter class of immigrants tended to bring their families and relatives with them, contributing to the growth of the Indian population in the city.

By the middle of the 19th century, Singapore also saw a third group of Indian migrants, comprising commercial classes and mainly consisting of Chettiars, a Tamil community of businessmen and financiers who became well known as providers of credit to the whole business community in Singapore. In the early years of the 20th century, this commercial class expanded to include North Indian businessmen compromising Parsis, Sindhis, Sikhs, Marwaris and Gujaratis. These businessmen established themselves as wholesalers and retailers and, leveraging the worldwide trading networks of the Indian diaspora, helped Singapore grow into a global heart of commerce.

Such unconstrained Indian migration into Singapore ended in 1953, when two acts were passed that restricted the entry of Indians into Malaya and Singapore, especially as applied to unskilled labour. So, it was only in the final years of the 20th century, when immigration policy was eased, that yet another wave of Indians migrated to Singapore. Many of them came with superb educational and professional qualifications, including lawyers, doctors, journalists, teachers and technical personnel. Many of them are playing leading roles in the universities and research centres that will drive Singapore's next phase of growth. Where the original Indian migrants were mainly from the southern states of India and Punjab, this later group is much more heterogeneous.

Indians Left an Imprint on Economic Policy

Some Singapore Indians have also played major roles in economic development policy. Although not an economist, former Foreign Minister and Deputy Prime Minister Mr. Sinnathamby Rajaratnam came up with the concept of Singapore as a global city in 1972, well before it became the fashion to talk about global cities. Rajaratnam outlined a case for why, at that time, Singapore could no longer rely on remaining as a key trading hub and marketplace in Southeast Asia. He had spotted the new emerging trends driven by advances in shipping (such as containerisation), developments in communications technology, the growing network of financial centres around the world and the internationalisation of production as multinational companies re-modelled their business operations. We take these factors for granted these days, but they were not so obvious 40 years ago. Rajaratnam understood that these new trends explained why Singapore's air and shipping links with the wider global economy were growing strongly, whereas the traditional regionally based entrepôt trade was losing momentum. Consequently, he persuasively argued that Singapore's future lay in becoming a major node in the global economic system as a global city. Today, as a result of Rajaratnam's foresight and the policies that came out of that, Singapore is one of the major global cities of the world.

Another giant in economic policy planning is Mr. J.Y. Pillay. An engineer by training, he was once described by Lee Kuan Yew as being "equal to the best brains in America." Mr. Pillay played a key role in shaping the economy during modern Singapore's early years, from managing the withdrawal of the British troops in the early 1970s to formulating the country's tax policy. In the crucial years of Singapore's economic development, he supervised critical ministries, including Finance and National Development. He was also managing director of the Monetary Authority of Singapore (MAS) and of the Government of Singapore Investment Corporation. Not only did he oversee virtually all of the important economic agencies, his biggest contribution was building Singapore Airlines from a staff of just 12 in 1972 to being the world-class carrier that it is today.

What of the Future? Indians Likely to Step up their Contributions

The role Indians will play in Singapore's economy is set to grow as India regains its place as one of the largest economies in the world. With the right policies, India is likely to grow at more than 7% a year for the foreseeable future, to emerge by the late 2030s as the second-largest economy in the world. As India's economy takes off, Singapore has an eminently good chance of becoming, first, India's main window to the rest of the world, and second, the premier gateway into India. Indians here will help Singapore achieve these roles, as they can leverage their language skills, their cultural understanding of India and their networks in India.

Already Singapore accounts for about a fifth of outbound foreign direct investments from companies in India, making it one of the most preferred places for Indian-based companies looking to invest and expand their operations overseas. Many of India's biggest corporations perceive Singapore as the next big step in the global expansion of their businesses. Recently, Tata Communications set up a S$210 million data centre and telecommunications facility here and plans to invest a further S$440 million over the next few years. Indian-owned businesses in Singapore have multiplied four-fold to over 4000 since 2001.

Singapore is also a major gateway into India — its air and shipping hubs provide multiple access routes into all of the top-tier cities, as well as many emerging urban conurbations in India. Large equity funds investing in India tend to use Singapore as a base for such investment. Singapore's Closer Economic Cooperation Agreement with India has also made Singapore the hub from which global investors channel their foreign direct investments into India.

Conclusion

Despite their relatively small share of the population, Indians have played a significant role in Singapore's economy over the years. This role has been an evolving one, with contributions being made across the spectrum of economic activities, from manual labour to research and development. Furthermore, with India's unstoppable economic rise, Indians here will be able to play an even larger role in the future.

Manu Bhaskaran is Director of Centennial Group International and the Founding Director and Chief Executive Officer of Centennial Asia Advisors. Mr. Bhaskaran has more than 30 years of expertise in economic and political risk assessment and forecasting in Asia. Before joining the Centennial Group, he was Chief Economist for Asia of a leading international investment bank and managed its Singapore-based economic advisory group. Mr. Bhaskaran is a well-regarded commentator on Asian financial and economic affairs, and has regular columns in business weeklies such as the Edge in Singapore/Malaysia. He serves as Member of the Regional Advisory Board for Asia of the International Monetary Fund; Senior Adjunct Fellow, Institute of Policy Studies; Council Member of the Singapore Institute of International Affairs; and Vice-President of the Economics Society of Singapore. Mr. Bhaskaran has a Master's degree in Public Administration from the John F. Kennedy School of Government at Harvard University and a Bachelor's degree in economics from Cambridge University. He has also qualified as a Chartered Financial Analyst. He is based in Singapore.

11 Less Remembered Spaces and Interactions in a Changing Singapore: Indian Business Communities in the Post-independence Period

Jayati Bhattacharya

A significant milestone in the Singapore–India bilateral relations was achieved when tourists from Singapore were allowed 'visa-on-arrival' by the Indian government in 2010 on a unilateral basis. This further enhanced the mobility of people between the two states, the momentum for which had already begun more than a decade ago. Interestingly, the visa requirements for mutual travel were only introduced in the 1980s,[1] which meant that the colonial conjunctions that had been created in the 19th and 20th centuries flowed into the post-independence era bearing strong footsteps of a legacy, and had not disappeared at any point of time. One of the less visible of these legacies was the existence of the Indian business communities[2] in the changing landscape of Singapore in the post-1965 phase. This article will attempt to throw some light on the changing roles, sustenance and progress of these communities in the larger framework of Singapore's success story.

The Indian business communities in Singapore have not been a part of the popular academic discourse in spite of the fact that they had been an inevitable part of the British imperial project right from the time of Raffles' landing on this island city,[3] along with one Narayan Pillai. Pillai, an interpreter and businessman, who played a significant role in laying the foundation of modern Singapore. However, Indian businessmen and trading groups operated on the margins of the colonial economic order, in alignment with the colonial circulation of men and money, rarely coming into conflict with hegemonic power dictations. One obvious reason for lesser visibility was the overwhelming demographic domination of the labouring migrants from the Indian subcontinent to the Malayan peninsula. The other possible reason for their exclusion from the prisms of Western discourse could be the complexities and heterogeneities that existed among these communities. However, some groups, like the Chettiars, were facilitated by the colonial powers in their mobility for financing imperial ambitions. Other important Indian regional business groups were Gujaratis, Sindhis, Punjabis, Parsis, Chulias, Moplahs, Mudaliars and Vellalars, to name some of them. In spite of being minorities amongst the demographic minority of Indians in Singapore, these business communities made for a significant visible presence in the spatial landscape of colonial Singapore in areas like Market Street, Chulia Street, High Street and Serangoon Road, and continued with their imprints for more than a decade in post-independence Singapore, before gradually giving way to reconstructed spaces and new business paradigms.

The Post-Independence Period

Like many other communities in the post-1965 period, the Indian business groups too had to renegotiate their space and identity in the changing dynamics of the new state order. Thus, the established firms and business concerns went through different stages of "highs and lows, business changed hands, and the character of the goods and commodities of trade altered."[4] The colonial business districts and living spaces gradually gave way to the modern refurbished structures of

Chulia Street towards Market Street. Chulia Street towards Market Street near the Boat Quay area, 1982. B.S. Mohideen & Co. at 26, Chulia Street can be seen in the photograph. (From the Lee Kip Lin Collection. All rights reserved. Lee Kip Lin and National Library Board, Singapore 2009.)

a multi-racial, multi-ethnic Singapore, where new urban landscapes emerged, racially balanced living spaces in the form of Housing Development Board (HDB) flats were developed, communication facilities were built and new manufacturing units were set up. The government embarked on a period of import substitution in the 1960s, followed by export-orientated industrialisation in the late 1970s and early 1980s. Multinational enterprises were involved to integrate foreign expertise and technological know-how in the growth process, making the domestic market extremely competitive for small- and medium-level businesses. Regional patterns of trading, in which most of the Indian firms were engaged, had to be reorganised in light of the post-colonial order, the Cold War tremors and the *Konfrontasi* issues in the neighbouring region. Numerous small- and medium-level Indian business firms, having lost customers in the region, faced great financial crises and some-times went bankrupt in the 1970s. Migration laws and money-lending policies had also changed in the new scenario, thus striking a blow to the traditional Chettiar financing activities. Over the decades, the Chettiars gradually opted for higher education and different professions, with many of them eventually choosing to migrate to the West. The Urban (Ceiling and Regulation) Act and the Rent Control Act also turned the tide against many of the existing propertied businessmen and landowners. A closer look at the spaces and people involved with business provides us with glimpses of the prevailing situation then.

Business, Landscape and People

High Street

The appearance of the present-day High Street gives little idea of a completely different structural space in the same area in the colonial and early post-colonial period. The area was then lined with shops, mostly of two or three floors — the ground floor used for retail, whereas the upper floor was used for wholesale and export–import businesses. They were represented mostly by traders and merchants from North India, like the Sindhis, Punjabis and Gujaratis. One account of oral history recordings tells us that there were more than 50 shops participating in retail and wholesale businesses and more than 500 businessmen engaged in the wholesale business of textiles. These numbers reduced down to 50/60 textile shops by 1985.[5] The figures might have been over-estimated to a certain extent; however, they reflect the magnitude of business interactions in the area in living memory. At a time when Orchard Road was yet to develop as a popular retail–shopping destination, High Street in the 1960s and 1970s was a fashionable place to shop. There are also stories of lively Diwali (Deepavali) celebrations in the area,[6] suggesting a greater presence and interaction of Indians

Rows of shophouses along High Street in 1982. (From the Lee Kip Lin Collection. All rights reserved. Lee Kip Lin and National Library Board, Singapore 2009.)

in this predominantly business space. On other occasions, like the National Day celebrations, the Singapore Indian Chamber of Commerce put up an illuminated arch across High Street in the name of the Chamber.[7]

Singapore had served as a centre for entrepôt trade in textiles, where textile products arrived from different parts of the globe to be redistributed to other parts of Southeast Asia. Indians, mainly the Gujaratis, Punjabis and Sindhis, were mostly involved in this trading activity, almost in a monopolistic manner, with connections extending to their own distribution networks in the hinterland in different parts of Southeast Asia. This remained as one of the most popular and lucrative businesses for them throughout the 1970s. They were actively engaged in outward-bound trading activities and regional distribution networks. A part of their business activities was also catering to the retail necessities of the domestic market, which was much smaller than the regional markets. However, the post-colonial nation-building processes in different emerging nation states hindered smooth operations of an ethnic community-based business transactions. The new states in the post-colonial order were also building up their own textile manufacturers and thus imposed restrictions on the traditional regional trading practices, bringing about a decline of the concerned firms. The sensitive relations of Singapore with its neighbours in this period also dampened existing business relations. With profit margins and

Shophouses along High Street. The Wassiamulls were a prominent presence in 1982. (From the Lee Kip Lin Collection. All rights reserved. Lee Kip Lin and National Library Board, Singapore 2009.)

business volumes receding at a fast pace, many of the players opted to retire and shut down their businesses, or look for other alternatives.

While a large number of medium and small north Indian trading groups petered out, there were others who not only survived and progressed, but also successfully diversified into different sectors and spread their wings outside Singapore as well. Some of the popular, big names of the period that continued their flourishing business activities beyond Singapore were the Kewalram Chanrai Group, the Thakrals, the Jumabhoys, the Tolarams, the Royal Brothers Group and Pars Ram Brothers, to name a few of them.[8] Others business groups, like the Chhotirmals, either chose to reduce their operations in Singapore and/or migrate to Hong Kong.

While the globe-trotting Chanrais have been active in businesses involving textiles, silk and curios in Singapore and other parts of Southeast Asia since the 1920s, they finally consolidated their global ventures in Singapore in 1976 with the establishment of 'Kewalram Singapore', and eventually diversified into distribution and manufacturing. They are commonly associated with their well-known offshoot, 'Olam International'.[9]

Tolarams, on the other hand, established their Singapore office in 1965, which is now the headquarters of the group. They expanded outwards with their first green-field textile manufacturing plant in Indonesia in 1973 and entered into the

Rows of shophouses along High Street, from Hill Street Corner, 1982. (From the Lee Kip Lin Collection. All rights reserved. Lee Kip Lin and National Library Board, Singapore 2009.)

African market in 1976, and later spread to Estonia in 1995, becoming one of the first Singaporean companies to do so. They dealt with diverse products ranging from electronics, consumer goods, paper, instant noodles, chemical and dyestuffs, etc.

Another popular name in Indian business was the Jumabhoys. While Rajabali Jumabhoy had been a prominent name since the 1920s, and was also actively associated with building up the Indian Chamber of Commerce and negotiating with the British government on various trade issues, the family business faced internal feuds and conflicts later in the post-independence period. In 1975, the family residence at Scotts Road was developed as a commercial complex, and the

Scotts Shopping Centre, the Ascott serviced apartments and the Scott Holdings decided to go public in 1991.

The diversified business interests that emerged after 1965 were in consumer electronics, properties and hospitality businesses, as well as in the tourism sector. The Thakrals made a significant mark in consumer electronics, financial and investment services, hotels and tourism-based services that spread across the globe. They were one of the earliest business concerns from Singapore to establish contact with China in as early as the 1960s, and then set up their first office in 1984. The Thakrals also brought Japanese television sets into the Indian markets in the 1980s. There were others, like Shankar's Emporium Pte Ltd, a popular name in High Street throughout the 1980s and 1990s, who were active in consumer electronic goods and household appliances.

Market Street

Historically speaking, the interactive space of the Market Street area, in close proximity to the Singapore River as well as Raffles Place, is popularly associated with the overwhelming presence of the Chettiar community and their *kittangis* (Chettiar business centres structured in shop houses), which served as a space for both conducting their daily business as well as their residences. According to one source, at one point in time, there were about seven *kittangis* on Market Street

Shophouses with full-length French windows on Market Street, 1968. (From the Lee Kip Lin Collection. All rights reserved. Lee Kip Lin and National Library Board, Singapore 2009.)

Unrestored shophouses at the convergence of Cecil (left) and Market (right) Streets, 1967. (From the Lee Kip Lin Collection. All rights reserved. Lee Kip Lin and National Library Board, Singapore 2009.)

housing more than 300 companies. Market Street was also known as *Chetty Theruvu* or Chetty Street in Tamil. Frugal and simple in appearance, the Chettiars were an important trading and money-lending caste from Tamil Nadu in South India and one of the most affluent of the Indian communities in Southeast Asia. They were involved in financing trade, personal loans, etc., to all of those who were unable or unwilling to approach big European or Chinese banks. There was meticulous maintenance of records, unique accounting methods and interesting alignments of business with religion, thus building up a close association with the community's temple.

Since the Chettiars were closely tied to the colonial economy and finances, many began to return to India with the Second World War, and to an increasing degree after the British withdrawal. Their money-lending activity was circumscribed within a close-knit caste group, thus having little choice in diversification in the post-independence period. However, many of the firms continued their activities well into the 1970s until the *kittangis* had to be vacated for urban restructuring, and by the 1980s, the few remaining in the money-lending profession moved to the shop-house building near their temple in Tank Road, the Arulmigu Sri Thanday-uthapani Temple or, more popularly, the Subramaniam Temple. The Sithi Vinayagar Temple at Keong Saik Road has also been managed by the Chettiars since 1925.

Nostalgic reminders of the Chettiar presence and activities can be seen in the many names of the streets and lanes across the island, like Arnasalam Chetty

49, Market Street Kitangi — before demolition, 1977, S.Subbiah.
(Source: National Archives of Singapore.)

Road, Muthuraman Chetty Road, Narayanan Chetty Road, Annamalai Avenue and Meyyappa Chettiar Road. The lone *kittangi* that stands to this day is the Nagarathar Building, which had also served as the Chettiar Chambers of Commerce since the 1930s. The façade remains, but the thriving pulse of their businesses has receded into the memory of the older generations of Singapore.

Serangoon Road

The only living space that bears familiarity to the past imageries is the Serangoon Road area, more popularly known as Little India at present. This was a space where the market interactions were markedly different from other spaces. This space grew

V.K. Kalyanasundaram & Sons was a popular retail shop in Serangoon Road, 1982.
(Source: National Archives of Singapore.)

out of the necessity of catering to the daily requirements of a South Asian way of life. Thus, there was colour, aroma, sound, vibrancy and a unique thrive connecting the daily provisions, vegetables and fruits, cooked foods, hand-ground spices, fresh flowers, jewellery, textiles and clothing, music, traditional handicrafts and artifacts and similar things. Besides the large number of people who were engaged in retail businesses and general provisions, there were also others involved in wholesale businesses of textiles and spices. Though much has changed over the decades, the inner core of Little India has been maintained and conserved in a manner that can effectively transport oneself to a familiar space in South India. The government has successfully made efforts to promote tourism and preserve cultural memories, spaces and architecture in this area.

One popular name that resonated in the Serangoon Road area in the past was that of P. Govindasamy Pillai, or 'PGP' as he is fondly remembered, who had a number of PGP shops in the area selling various products since the colonial days. He started his first shop, Dhanalakshmi Stores, selling spices, oils and grains in the 1930s, and then expanded his business into textile shops, spices and flour mills. PGP stores were also opened in Johor and Malacca. He also owned properties in Serangoon Road, Buffalo Road and Race Course Road. Some of his shops stood in the same place where Little India Arcade is now located.[10] He was also a philanthropist, generously donating to the community in various ways. His

Clive Street, Little India area, 1982. (From the Lee Kip Lin Collection. All rights reserved. Lee Kip Lin and National Library Board, Singapore 2009.)

sons took his business forward, especially his eldest son, G. Ramachandran, who not only became a popular leader of the Indian community, but also diversified his father's textile and sundry goods businesses into wholesale trade in spices and also petroleum business. Though he lost substantial money and properties in business, spices proved to be most lucrative for him in the early 1970s.[11] Ramachandran also became the youngest president of the Singapore Indian Chamber of Commerce and Industry in 1966 and continued to lead the chamber for many years during the 1960s, 1970s and 1980s.

Other popular retail shops in the area were M.R.P. K. Vandayar & Sons, Sithi Vinayagar and V.K. Kalyanasundaram Stores. Kalyanasundaram had a number of shops in Buffalo Road, Dunlop Street and Serangoon Road. First-generation businessmen started most of these shops selling textiles, electronic goods, cosmetics and various other consumer goods. They provided food and lodging to their employees as well. Business thrived quite prosperously until the 1980s, when the businesses began facing tough competition from an emerging giant in the area, Mustafa. Unable to diversify and adapt in the small domestic market, most of these names phased out into oblivion.

However, Mohamed Mustafa & Shamsuddin Co., more popularly known as 'Mustafa', was a major exception. Hailing from a village in eastern Uttar Pradesh in Northern India, Haji Mohamed Mustafa opened his 500-square foot shop in Campbell

Lane in 1971 after initial days of struggle. Business prospered, but was disrupted in 1985 when his shops were acquired for conservation purposes. Undeterred, he went on to rent a space in the Serangoon Plaza, and soon began a major buying spree in Syed Alwi Road. His business expanded by leaps and bounds, transforming it into one of the dominant retail players in Singapore. Some other prominent names that prospered during this period were Sofeene Enterprises, popularly known as the Haniffas, and Jothi Stores and Flowers Shop (JSFS). Starting as small textile agents in 1970, Haniffa Shariff and Ally Shariff of Sofeene Enterprises expanded into carpets, fabrics and fibres in the 1980s and cotton, leather, paper, agricultural products and others in the 21st century.[12] A similar success story is that of JSFS, which was initially started in 1960 by Murugaia Ramachandra as a small shop selling betel leaves and other sundry items. The shop expanded, capitalising on the rituals and necessities of the religious mind-set of the Indian community and supplying flowers and garlands to the Indian temples. Ramachandra's son, Rajakumar, joined the business in 1985, diversifying the business to many Indian consumer products and rapidly expanding it.

Any discussion of Serangoon Road remains incomplete without mention of the restaurants and gold jewellery shops. Both the restaurants and gold jewellery shops were much fewer in number in the 1960s than what we see at present. However, there was a large number of goldsmiths in the area that were attached to the few gold shops and also catering individually to clients. The jewellery designs were typically hand-made and customised to suit the tastes and necessities of individual clients. One of the oldest names that still survives (though ownership has changed) is that of Ani Mani Porchalai, as well as a family of goldsmiths of three generations represented in Muthukrishnan's Mukuthi Corner. Dawood Maraikar & Sons was another big name in this business in the 1960s. Over the decades, most of the goldsmiths returned to India, while old gold shops changed hands. One of the earliest Chinese shops in the area was that of Batu Pahat, which became a training ground for many of the future owners of shops in the area. I have discussed the transition of the gold jewellery business in Little India in more detail in a different article.[13]

Similarly, the growth and development of Indian restaurants in the Serangoon Road area deserves a separate study altogether. Housing some of the very modest restaurants in the area since colonial days, like Komala Vilas and Ananda Bhavan, and catering to the daily necessities of food for the shop-house residents in the community, the scene has changed since the 1980s. "From the 1980s, there has developed an interest in various Indian cuisines among the non-Indian community as well and entrepreneurs were quick to exploit the fondness for spicy food, Singaporean and foreign."[14] Restaurants like The Banana Leaf Apolo, Muthu's Curry, etc., followed by many more specialised restaurants in the new century, catered to this new kind of emerging taste, soon turning Race Course Road into a hub of Indian eateries of various cuisines.

Interactions with the Indian Economy

A significant development of Singapore-India bilateral ties, progress of the Indian economy and changes in the local scenario have been witnessed, particularly from the 1990s onwards. By contrast, between the 1960s and 1980s, the economic transition of Indian businesses in local spaces was quite independent of any bilateral interactions. The reason for this was quite obvious. India and Singapore followed different trajectories of economic growth, and converging interests were difficult between the free-market economy of Singapore and the domestic-centric, inward-looking Indian economy. Nevertheless, diplomatic exchanges continued, with Lee Kuan Yew visiting India quite a few times during this period and trade dialogues being held, but there were no substantial achievements when compared to the forthcoming decades. Interestingly, two proposals from India for setting up factories in Singapore from Messrs. Kesoram Industries & Cotton Mills Ltd., Calcutta, for the manufacture of transparent paper, and another from Universal Engineering Works from Rajkot for a machine tool factory, were placed through the Singapore Indian Chamber's Industrial Sub-Committee in 1968.[15] Not much is heard about either of these proposals later, but it is interesting to see the interest of these very local business entities in investing in Singapore. However, the significant entry of one of the biggest corporate houses in India, the Tatas, into Singapore and their participation in Singapore's technological progress during this period has often been ignored and marginalised. Tata Motors, Tata International AG along with the help of DBS promoted Tata Precision Industries Pte Ltd in 1972 and also started the Tata Government Training Centre.[16] This was a ground-breaking venture headed by the much-acclaimed loyal Tata engineer, Syamal Gupta, both from the perspective of an Indian business concern at a time of discouraging domestic regulations and pessimistic outward investments, as well as from the point of view of Singapore in incorporating an Indian concern for its manufacturing advancement and progress. There was also another big business house of India, Godrej, who made inroads into Southeast Asia during this time through Singapore and Malaysia. While their steel manufacturing plant was set up in Johor Bahru, Malaysia, 'Godrej, Singapore' was incorporated in 1972[17] and ran successfully for more than 30 years.

Conclusion

It is interesting to witness the differences in the characters of different Indian business spaces in the island-state in spite of the minority presence of Indian business communities in Singapore. This reveals the diversity and heterogeneity of the trading and merchant groups from India and different linguistic, financial and manpower networks within the popularly imagined homogenised identity.

The participation, diversification and transition of Indian businesses in Singapore in the post-1965 phase has quite often been overwhelmed by the engaging interactions of the Singapore–India relations since the liberalisation of the Indian economy in the 1990s and the Look East Policy that has ushered in enormous changes in business exchanges, diplomatic interactions and diasporic transitions. However, these changes have had foundations in the past transitions and have been torch-bearers for the future. The subsequent interactions, in spite of them being more policy-driven and much more voluminous in scope and effect, do reflect the circular and fluid movements of the past. The visa regulations might have changed in different periods of time, but the spirit of communication of men, money and materials resonated with the legacies of past exchanges, though in different dimensions. These issues will have been be discussed in another chapter on a more contemporary phase in this volume. Many of the business spaces and firms, as discussed above, have gone through complete transformations and paradigm shifts in a manner that bears little resemblance to the modern landscape of Singapore, but undoubtedly forms an inseparable and important heritage of the island-state and a significant part of its progress and development.

Select References

1. The visa requirement for Singapore citizens by India started in 1984 and was followed by Singapore, which introduced it in 1985. See https://www.hcisingapore.gov.in/pages.php?id=68, retrieved 24 February 2015.
2. I prefer to pluralise the Indian business communities due to the complexities and heterogeneities that exist within the same ethnic group.
3. The association of Indian trade and business with the Malayan peninsula and other parts of Southeast Asia was pre-colonial and much more deep-rooted.
4. Bhattacharya J. (2011). *Beyond the Myth: Indian Business Communities in Singapore*. Singapore, ISEAS, p. 91.
5. Kothari G. (n.d.). Oral History Recordings, Accession no. A000549, Reel no. 14, National Archives of Singapore.
6. Chhatru Vaswani, a Sindhi businessman and greatly involved with the Sindhi Association for many years in Singapore, in conversation with the author in May 2009.

7. *The SICCI Journey: 1924–2014 — Singapore Indian Chamber of Commerce and Industry.* Singapore, SICCI, 2014, pp. 31–32.

8. I have discussed each of these concerns in greater details in my book, *Beyond the Myth*, op. cit.

9. For further details, refer to the case study on the Chanrais in *Beyond the Myth*, pp. 258–274.

10. Arunasalam S. (n.d.). P. Govindasamy Pillai. http://eresources.nlb.gov.sg/infopedia/articles/SIP_262_2005-01-13.html, retrieved on 28 March 2015.

11. Bhattacharya J., op. cit., p. 102.

12. For further details, refer to Bhattacharya, *Beyond the Myth*, ibid., pp. 121–122.

13. Bhattacharya J. (2015). Beyond the glitterati: The Indian and Chinese jewellers of Little India. In: Bhattacharya J., Kripalani C. (ed) *Indian and Chinese Immigrant Communities: Comparative Perspectives.* London, Anthem-ISEAS.

14. Bhattacharya J., *Beyond the Myth*, p. 106.

15. *The SICCI Journey: 1924–2014 — Singapore Indian Chamber of Commerce and Industry*, p. 32.

16. Datta-Ray SK. (2010). *Looking East to Look West: Lee Kuan Yew's Mission India.* Singapore, ISEAS, pp. 194–197.

17. Karanjia BK. (1997). *The Builder also Grows: Godrej — A Hundred Years, 1897–1997, Volume II.* New Delhi, Viking by Penguin Books, pp. 211–212.

Jayati Bhattacharya is a lecturer in the South Asian Studies Programme at the National University of Singapore. She has research interests in business history, Indian trade diaspora, connected histories, South-Southeast Asian relations and Comparative Diasporas. Previously, she had been a Visiting Research Fellow at the Institute of Southeast Asian Studies (ISEAS) and continued her affiliation to the Institute as an Associate Fellow till April 2014. She is currently doing research on Singapore-India relations with the aim of publishing a monograph on the same. Her previous publications include *Beyond the Myth: Indian Business Communities in Singapore* (Singapore: ISEAS, 2011) which traces the origin, evolution and growth of the ethnic Indian business diaspora in Singapore and also gives an insight into the socio-economic dynamics and political initiatives in contemporary times; and co-edited volume with Oliver Pye, *The Palm Oil Controversy in Southeast Asia: A Transnational Perspective* (Singapore: ISEAS, 2012), which is a collection of papers on the oil palm and the global controversies surrounding it. Her recently co-edited volume with Coonoor Kripalani, *Indian and Chinese Immigrant Communities: Comparative Perspectives* (Anthem-ISEAS: London, 2015) focusses on the lived-spaces and interactions of the Indian and Chinese communities in different geopolitical contexts.

12 Newly Arrived Indian Professionals — Contributing to a Globalising Singapore

Girija Pande

On any given day at Raffles Place, Changi Business Park or any of Singapore's many commercial hubs, a stream of Indian professionals can be seen sauntering in executive wear or unwinding after office hours at the city's myriad watering holes. Many of these professionals are India's top talent, who have graduated from the best universities in India and abroad, and they now populate many key industries in Singapore, such as finance, technology and business services. Additionally, many professional areas, such as accounting, legal, medical and academia, have also hired talent from India so as to compete better in the rapidly globalising Singapore. Consequently, Indian professionals and knowledge workers now form a significant part of Singapore's growing global workforce. Like their counterparts in business centres in London or New York, over the last two decades, many of them have adopted Singapore as their home, and so they constitute an important thread in the fabric of Singapore's society.

Nearly two centuries ago, Chettiars from South India were a prominent group of commercial migrants whose financial skills oiled the wheels of commerce in colonial Singapore. They successfully provided the skills needed at that time. Similarly, today's professionals from India come armed with the 21st century skills needed by a new and more global Singapore.

Making Singapore Home

Highly skilled Indian professionals are part of a growing non-resident Indian (NRI) diaspora, now totalling around 30 million and settled in many parts of the world. They have been actively sought by global MNCs for the last four decades. Today, many have made their mark in these Western organisations, with some having succeeded and become CEOs. Names like Indira Nooyi in Pepsico, Vikram Pandit in Citibank and Satya Nadella in Microsoft are of course well known as CEOs of these iconic giants. In the mid-1990s, the opening up of India to global opportunities led to Singapore's developing interest. Indian professionals who usually looked to the West to emigrate were increasingly attracted to Singapore due to its Asian heritage, closeness to India, its image as an exceptionally well-governed country and the fact that it was a meritocracy. For those from the Indian state of Tamilnadu, the added attraction was the use of Tamil, one of the national languages of Singapore. The wry answer to "Why Singapore?" was very often "What's not to like about Singapore?" Indian professionals who settled in Singapore saw the benefits of the existing Indian heritage, Indian schools and educational institutions and the sights and smells of Little India and the Mustafa Shopping Centre, which reminded them of home. It is therefore not surprising that within two decades, very much like in the West, Indian professionals took on very senior positions in Singaporean companies and MNCs. Piyush Gupta helms DBS Group and Sunny Varghese is at Olam International, whilst Harish Munwani was global COO of Unilever worldwide, based in Singapore, and Gautam Bannerji headed PWC in Singapore for many years.

> The history of Indian professionals in Singapore symbolises the ever-strengthening relationship between India and Singapore. It has led to Singapore's growing interest in a modernising India and its widely scattered and successful skilled professionals. Singapore started recruiting Indian technology talents in the early 1990s when its immigration policies were liberalised to attract foreign professionals in order to boost the size and skills of its own workforce. The government was keen to attract well-educated immigrants from Asian countries and it was hoped that they would sink their roots and offset the low fertility rates of the resident population.

The 2010 census put the total Singapore Indian resident population at around 350,000 (i.e. 9.2% of the total population, an increase of nearly 3% since the census of three decades ago in 1980). This included nearly 110,000 Indian permanent residents (PRs), the majority of whom were highly qualified Indian professionals based in Singapore. If one adds to this the many professionals who have readily accepted becoming Singaporean citizens, one could easily put this number to nearly 150,000 Indian professionals today who have made Singapore their home in the last 25 years — that is, half the period in which Singapore has been independent. The growing membership of Indian professionals in various prestigious alumni associations in Singapore is evidence enough of this large influx. The Indian Institutes of Technology (IIT), Indian Institutes of Management (IIM) and Chartered

Accountants Institute of India produce the *crème de la crème* of Indian graduates, and each association of such professionals in Singapore has a membership exceeding 1000 each. In fact, they often boast of having the largest single-city presence outside India, which is testament to Singapore's appeal amongst such qualified Indian professionals!

Growth of Businesses

The signing of the historic Comprehensive Economic Cooperation Agreement (CECA) in 2005 between India and Singapore was the catalyst that made many major Indian business groups use Singapore as their international headquarters as these companies sought to globalise their operations beyond India and build businesses in the Asia–Pacific and China. Major Indian groups like Tata, Birla and Punj Lloyd set up many of their subsidiaries in Singapore and brought with them their best skills. Some of these companies even acquired iconic Singaporean companies like Natsteel and Sembawang Engineers to get scale. Tata Group's connection with Singapore goes back to 1972, when Tata Precision set up a precision instruments plant and a joint government training centre in order to train Singaporeans in precision engineering as Singapore industrialised. Well-known technology giants like Tata Consultancy Services, Infosys, WIPRO and Tech Mahindra soon set up Asia–Pacific offices, which permitted them to expand into the ever-growing hinterland of Singapore. Today, there are over 6000 Indian companies based in Singapore, the largest number from any country. While many of them remain small entrepreneurial trading companies, nearly 100 Indian companies are significantly entrenched in terms of size and scale in Singapore.

The steady growth of Singapore's commercial and investment ties with India, along with the arrival of Indian companies in Singapore, led to the increase in the talent pool of Indian professionals in Singapore since 2008. This was the time when the Western markets were adversely impacted by the global financial crisis and many Indian professionals who were employed there found Singapore to be a growing and global financial centre where they could use their sophisticated talents in the finance and information technology industries. This resulted in the growth of senior global bankers, wealth and asset managers, hedge funds, foreign exchange/bond dealers and private equity professionals, who made Singapore their home and contributed to Singapore's growth as a well-recognised global financial centre. A similar situation existed in other professional fields, such as academia, accounting, medicine, law and engineering, where newly arrived Indians have made their mark in their respective professions in Singapore. In addition, Bangalore and Silicon Valley-based Indian technology professionals were attracted to Singapore as a centre for incubating new technology companies, as Singapore positioned itself as a centre for start-ups in information technology, biosciences and pharmaceuticals. The globalising of Singapore and upscaling of its industry to knowledge-based ones provided desirable challenges for professionals of this calibre. It was a great fit and a win–win for both: Singapore acquired global talent that could easily sink their roots within the community, whilst professionals had the benefit of staying and working in an Asian city that was not only close to home, but also functioned exceedingly well and believed in meritocracy.

Integration Challenge

The sudden influx of large numbers of immigrants from all over Asia into Singapore has also had some unintended consequences, and a response to this has been a clamour for slowing down the pace of inducting foreigners into Singapore, including Indian professionals. Some have seen their PR or citizenship applications denied, unlike the situation a decade ago. The image of Indian professionals and wealthy Indian businessmen who have made Singapore their home is generally a benign one in Singapore society. They are considered model immigrants — law abiding, industrious and relatively high tax-paying residents who have contributed greatly to the growth of the Singaporean economy and helped sustain Singapore's status as a global city. Often, however, their income levels are subject to public scrutiny. A recent *Straits Times* article on the income levels of all PRs indicated that the income data of ethnic Indian Singaporeans is inflated by lumping them together with India-born professional PRs who are often better educated. In 2010, the average income from work in homes where the head of the household was of Indian origin was S$7664 — well above the national average of S$7214. Success at this scale often creates integration challenges with local society at large, and this is something Indian professionals have become aware of. This is not dissimilar to the situations in the UK and USA, where the Indian community has achieved some of the highest income levels and drawn public attention to their successes.

It is often said that the larger the pool of any nationality with similar characteristics, the greater the integration challenge with the wider society. Indian professionals in Singapore who have by now reached a certain scale tend to face similar challenges. Proximity to India, the availability of Indian schools, shops and movie theatres and the formation of individual societies from numerous states of India have created a comfortable surrounding that acts as a barrier to the larger goal of integration and sinking roots deeply into the local community. Moreover, the Singaporean Indian community, which has existed in Singapore for nearly two centuries with a deeply embedded Singaporean ethos, often finds itself to be different from these newly minted citizens from their home country. Many articles, writings and theatre productions have highlighted this fact, and a healthy debate will hopefully improve the integration of these newly arrived Indian professionals into the larger Singaporean society. Some initiatives are now underway to foster this assimilation. SINDA, the well-known self-help group catering to the uplifting of underprivileged Singaporean Indians through improvements in education, has taken it upon itself to create an outreach platform called the Indian Businessmen's Roundtable (IBR) for senior leaders of newly arrived Indian professionals, in which they could use their skills, connections and wealth for a variety of community causes. Similarly, the Indian Women's Association (IWA) has done very good work for the underprivileged elderly. The response to such initiatives has been very good, and many such platforms will need to be created in future in order to achieve deeper integration into Singaporean society.

Looking Ahead

As in all immigrant societies, it is the second generation of these Indian professionals who will gradually meld with the Singaporean society and add to its rich mosaic of many nationalities. They will be imbued with the ambition to succeed in such a competitive society as Singapore by their parents who struggled to succeed in an equally competitive Indian society. Their links with India, both personal and professional, will remain strong and will be unique assets for Singapore as India takes its place as the third-largest economy in the world in the coming decade. As Singapore's industry becomes more knowledge intensive and global, these second-generation children of Indian professionals will become even more useful citizens than their parents who preceded them. If one has to go by examples, second-generation American or British–Indian citizens are currently playing major roles both within their communities and by acting as bridges between their current homelands and the homeland that their parents belonged to. They are treated with great respect for their professionalism and entrepreneurship, and the land of their parents, India, looks to them as friends who will help develop business links and inter-personal ties. This is the soft power that India believes will bring benefits to it and its trade and commerce with a country like Singapore in the years to come.

By nurturing these children of Indian professionals who have chosen to make Singapore their home, Singapore has done exactly what it did two centuries ago when Indians from all walks of life came here to seek their fortune and, in the process, added much more to the local community. As Singapore celebrates its 50th year of independence, newly arrived Indian professionals will be joining their fellow citizens in celebrating the event with great joy and satisfaction.

Mr. Girija Pande is the Executive Chairman of Apex Avalon Consulting Pte Ltd, which provides Strategy Consultancy services in the Asia Pacific (APAC) region and is a joint venture with India's Avalon Group which is ranked in the top 10 in APAC in Strategy Consulting. Mr. Pande has spent over three decades across APAC in senior positions with ANZ Banking Group and Tata Consultancy Services (TCS) Ltd, a global IT company. In his last role as Chairman of TCS, he grew its APAC businesses from scratch to over 11,000 associates in 14 countries — including 2,500 in China. He was conferred the best CEO award in Singapore HR Institute. Mr. Pande served as Economic Advisor to the Mayor of Guangzhou. He serves on the Boards of a few listed and non listed Companies in Singapore and is on the Advisory Board of SMU, the boards of SICC and ISAS.

Mr. Pande has recently co authored a book published by John Wiley (USA) on growing commercial ties between India and China titled, *The Silk Road Rediscovered — How Indian and Chinese Companies Are Becoming Globally Stronger by Winning in Each Other's Markets*. The book has a foreword by the MD of Brookings Institution, Bill Antholis.

13 To Singapore with Love…

Uma Rajan

Indian women in Singapore have left their footprints firmly in Singapore's sands of time and history with their dedicated contribution to various forms of human activity and industry. Some of them are not with us today, but their contributions continue to benefit us. Others who are still with us continue to make significant contributions nationally and internationally in their respective fields of interest. We have political leaders, social activists, civil servants, social workers, community leaders, administrators, artists, doctors, lawyers, business entrepreneurs, journalists, athletes and many others who have proved that, despite all the odds being stacked against them, they can equal anyone else in every way. They have made a difference, enjoyed the support of their families and many have raised daughters and sons who have and still are contributing to Singapore's economy and society.

There is undoubtedly an increasing participation of Indian women, both Singapore citizens and permanent residents, in Singapore's economy. They have grown with the nation, received higher education and contributed to the country's economic development. Government, legislature, courts, social organisations and social efforts have created a level playing field for women through changes in laws and social mores. Flexi-work arrangements and support systems have reduced work–family conflict, addressed issues of childcare and encouraged women to enter and remain in the labour force. The environment is also able to offer exciting new challenges, opportunities for career paths and training and adequate financial remuneration. Indian women have also improved their lot by actively participating in non-governmental organisations in order to address matters of concern and create income-generating activities that bring them greater economic independence. Over the past five decades, there has been an increase in the number of Indian women holding administrative and managerial posts, technicians and associate professionals, clerical workers and sales workers.

Indian women, with their rich cultural background, have always enriched Singapore's multi-ethnic culture and helped build bridges between other local communities. They have encouraged and enabled the exchange of potential benefits and mutual recognition, leading to their acceptance and integration into Singaporean society. Their outstanding contributions have been in all aspects of human activity, including their own cultural heritage and their role as women in society. They have played a major role, as have other women, in the upbringing of their children — imparting good qualities, establishing Indian cultural values, being family centred, supporting and respecting filial piety and inculcating feelings for the community and the country.

Some Indian women have chosen not to pursue traditional corporate careers, and become entrepreneurs instead. Increasing numbers are venturing into running businesses motivated by better education, labour shortages, encouragement to achieve entrepreneurial success and to enjoy the resulting flexible lifestyle. They have entered diversified business fields, ranging from commodities to retail to electronics. Many of them have also moved on to become successful home operators, trading in everything from textiles, jewellery, fashion, food and beverages, handicrafts, gifts and accessories, home decor, beauty and bridal goods, healthcare, etc., and their future seems bright and hopeful.

Over the past two decades, increasing numbers of Indian diaspora women have contributed their knowledge and skills to Singapore's economic growth and competitiveness and benefitted the country's development. As transnationals, they have mobilised their cultural, economic and financial capital and trade to open up new markets and provide opportunities for investment. They have tapped into their extensive networks using social media, maintained relationships, helped identify opportunities to facilitate engagement in development and strengthened cultural, political and economic links.

Despite all of the problems faced, Indian women, comprising both low and highly skilled workers, have played an important role within the socio-economic fabric, holding professional and managerial positions in every possible industry. Society recognises their contribution towards the growth of the country's economy, no matter how small the contribution may be. They have helped to shape the Singapore we know today and contributed to the tremendous changes in Singaporean society over the past 50 years. They have established themselves successfully in Singapore as well as on the international stage, reflecting the quality and talent within the community.

We salute all Indian women, Singapore citizens and permanent residents, who, in their own way, are carrying the bread basket of their family. We record our deep admiration for these women who have, with their innate ability, balanced their multiple roles of home makers and career women. They have silently and softly enhanced their status and made great contributions to Singapore over the past 50 years. They definitely have cause to celebrate these 50 years, along with our nation's 50th anniversary.

Portrait Gallery of Eminent Indian Women

We are able to present a portrait gallery of eminent Indian women who have achieved remarkable successes and made outstanding contributions in every possible field of human activity over the past 50 years.

(a) Politics

Traditionally, Indian women in Singapore have played a small role in the country's political scene and public life. Notable female politicians include Dhanam Avadai, PAP Member for Moulmein (1965–1968), lawyer Indranee Rajah, the current Senior Minister of State, Ministry of Law and Ministry of Education, and Indian-origin politician Halimah Yacob, former Minister and current Speaker of Parliament.

(b) Female Empowerment

Nominated Members of Parliament (NMP) have also made contributions to Singapore's political landscape, as they represent a range of societal interests involved with female empowerment. Orthopaedic Surgeon Kanwaljit Soin was the first female NMP to put up a Family Violence Bill in 1995, and her proposals were included in amendments to the Women's Charter. Journalist Braema Mathiaparanam, a former NMP, is the President of the SEA and Pacific Region of the International Council on Social Welfare (ICSW), a global non-governmental organisation that seeks to advance social welfare, social development and social justice. Associate Professor Kalyani Mehta, a former NMP, advocates for social workers and senior citizens.

(c) Social and Community Services

Pioneering women's rights activist, Checha Davies, sold her house in Johor to fund the YWCA hostel for low-income women. She founded the first Indian–Ceylonese Club in 1931, later renamed the Lotus Club, which later merged with the Ladies' Union to form the Kamala Club, which functions to date. A pioneering medical social worker Daisy Vaithilingam established Singapore's first fostering scheme for children, secured financial aid for parents of mentally disabled children and set up the Singapore Association of Social Workers. Veteran activist Constance Singam fought against domestic violence, which led to such victims being given legal protection today. Ardent volunteers in the Asian Women's Welfare Association (AWWA) Vimala Kulasekaran and Leana Thambyah spearheaded various projects for the welfare of the elderly, the disabled and children with multiple disabilities. Indranee Elizabeth Nadeson was the recipient of the 2009 inaugural Outstanding Lifetime Volunteer Award for her service as a foster mother to 43 children from 1976 to 2008.

(d) Civil and Administrative Services

The first and only female Ambassador of Singapore Jaya Mohideen is also the only Indian woman to be appointed to the Singapore Administrative Service to date. Justice Judith Prakash is a member of the Sub-Committee on the Review of Arbitration Laws that led to the enactment of the International Arbitration Act (Cap 143). Ms. Juthika Ramanathan is the first CEO of the Supreme Court.

(e) Healthcare

Dr. Sivakami Devi was the Deputy Director of Medical Services, Primary Health Care and Health Education, and in the 1970s, headed the Singapore Family Planning and Population Board and Home Nursing Foundation (HNF). Dr. Vatsala is an Advisor on Transplantation to the Ministry of Health. Many other female Indian doctors have and continue to contribute as heads of various major divisions of the healthcare industry: Shanta Emmanuel (research and evaluation), Rose Vaithinathan (training and health education), Rilly Ray (polyclinics), K. Vijaya (youth preventative services) and the multi-tasking Uma Rajan, a medical doctor and the first Singaporean to graduate in Classical Indian Dance (Bharatha Natyam) from India who successfully and passionately straddles healthcare, the arts and community work to date.

(f) Performing Arts

Music

Indian women have distinguished themselves in a number of cultural fields, in-cluding contemporary and traditional Indian art forms. Leading violinist Sharada Shankar was the recipient of the Kala Ratna and Empress of Classical Music Awards, in addition to many other awards and felicitations from 1939 until the 1990s, being a sought-after musician whose contribution to the Indian classical music scene on stage and in the media is unparalleled to date. Rani Singam was one of Asia's most sought-after singers and is named in 'The Jazz Singers', an encyclopaedia of important jazz vocalists. Her debut album *'With a Song in my Heart'*, by the legendary Jeremy Monteiro, is distributed in Asia and the United States. Jacintha Abisheganaden is an accomplished Singapore actress, entertainer and jazz singer who gained international recognition for her unique interpretations of jazz classics. Lalitha Vaidyanathan was Creative Director and Conductor of the Singapore Indian Orchestra and Choir owing to her passionate involvement in the development of an Indian orchestra that spanned all genres of Indian music. Shobha Shankar was the first and only Singapore Indian singer to sing a hit song for the Oscar-awarded music director A.R. Rahman, which was top of the Philips Top Ten for more than a year.

Dance

Cultural Medallionists Neila Sathyalingam (Founder and Artistic Director of Apsaras Arts Dance Company) and Santha Bhaskar (Artistic Director of Bhaskar's Arts Academy) are recognised for their outstanding services to Indian classical and multi-ethnic dance forms. They have both become synonymous with unique choreographies and concepts that combine the sophistication of traditional Indian dance and the innovative spirit of cross-cultural exploration. Cultural Medallionist Madhavi Krishnan greatly contributed to the National Theatre Dance Company and is remembered for her role as a favourite South Indian film comedienne. Others who have contributed in their own ways towards keeping the classical dance form alive include dance teachers Usha Rani Maniam, Vasantha Kasinath, Kesavan Sisters, Mohana Harendran and Indian classical dancers Rathi Karthigesu, Priyalatha Arun, Roshni Pillay and many others. Kavitha Krishnan, Creative Director of the Maya Dance Theatre, is an occupational therapist and a classical dancer who has successfully moved into the creation of an Asian contemporary dance style.

Literature

Writer Mera Chand, Chair for the Commonwealth Writers Prize for South East Asia and the South Pacific, is the recipient of the Special Recognition Award from MICA Singapore in 2011.

Visual Arts

'Conceptual artist' Kumari Nahappan is the recipient of many national and international awards, as well as the Indian Icon of the Year award winner of 2014. She combines painting, sculpture and installation works. Her iconic sculptures can be seen in landmark locations in Singapore and worldwide.

Museum Curators

Centre Director of the Indian Heritage Centre Dr. Gauri Parimoo Krishnan helped the South Asia collection in the Asian Civilisation Museum grow from a handful of objects to over 300 artefacts within 10 years. She curated key blockbuster exhibitions, spearheaded research projects and authored books on the Nalanda Trail and Ramayana.

The arts scene is developing many new talents among Indian diaspora women, especially in dance, music, the visual arts and handicrafts. Some run their own schools or classes in various community centres or even in their own homes, leading to a revival of interest and the raising of standards of the performing and other arts.

(g) Sports

Although Indian women's involvement in sports is not very prominent, we have had some notable achievements in the field of athletics. Glory Barnabas, a national sprinter, is remembered for her stunning 200 m gold medal victory at the 1973 SEAP Games and has won a gold and a silver medal in the women's 70–74 years age-group high jump and long jump, respectively, in 2013 at the International Gold Masters in Kyoto, Japan. K. Jayamani is a marathoner runner who won the women's title gold medal at the SEA Games in Singapore in 1983.

(h) Cuisine

Culinary consultant and recipe developer Devagi Sanmugam founded 'Epicurean World', a food consultancy business that combines her expert knowledge of gourmet cuisine with training programmes and many other culinary services.

(i) Fashion

Huri and Kavita Thulasidas are trendsetters of Indian fashion through Stylemart, the most recognised name in Singapore's Indian fashion landscape. They present a fusion of Asian cultures in their designs, with clients from among the elite in Singapore and beyond — including heads of state and members of royalty.

(j) Beauty

Sivarani runs Rupinis, the first Indian award-winning health and beauty institute offering skin and body treatment for women. A woman of immense courage as a breast cancer survivor, she raises awareness of breast cancer through her Divine Pink Events.

(k) Events Management

Purnima Kamath started De Ideaz Pte Ltd, an integrated marketing communications company, and successfully blended creativity and technology in order to promote events, entertainment, education and e-businesses to the social and corporate world.

(l) Journalism and Print Media

Shobha Tsering Bhalla is a Print media entrepreneur with the iconic status of a CEO of 'India Se', a leading lifestyle magazine for NRIs in Singapore.

(m) Education

Since colonial times, teaching has been a job at which Indian women have been well represented at all levels. As school principals and teachers, their contributions to the education services cannot be forgotten, as they have provided a continuous, seamless contribution towards the total development of schoolchildren.

Dr. Uma Rajan BBM, PBM, PBS. A doctor by profession and a graduate of Indian Classical Dance, Dr. Uma Rajan has been actively involved and is well known for her contributions to health care as Director, School Health and Elder Care Services of the Ministry of Health as well as her involvement in the arts, community and social service sectors in various capacities as Advisor, Board Member, Chairman, etc. She was lauded by the Prime Minister in his National Day Rally speech in 2014 for her introduction of the School Health Booklet for all students at school entry in the 1980s.

She is the first Singaporean to study dance formally in India from 1949 and returned as a graduate of Indian Classical Dance and awarded many titles. Also trained in Carnatic Music she was a regular performer over the Radio, TV and the stage. A choreographer for the Arts Festivals, the University and arts organisations, she was a charter Board Member of the National Arts Council when it was formed in 1990. During her tenure in NAC, she chaired all the three highly successful Festivals of Asian Performing Arts.

She sits on a wide range of Committees in Ministries, Statutory Boards, Community and other organisations. She has authored two books — both fund raising — the first *A Life For Others* on the extraordinary Buddhist nun Ven Ho Yuen Ho and a Cookbook *Spice Potpourri* in 2011, which won the 2012 World Gourmand Best Indian Cuisine Book and Best Fund Raising, Charity and Community Cookbook. A recipient of a wide range of awards both National and Community — the most recent being the 2011 National Day Honours — the Public Service Star Award — BBM and the Community Service Champion Award in 2015.

She actively pursues her interest in the arts and culture, social and community and health care sectors in her own way using her own formula.

14 Pakistanis in Singapore

Sajjad Ashraf

In 1947, when India was carved up in order to make Pakistan, millions who moved across the new dividing line are now called Indians. In 1971, when East Pakistan seceded to become Bangladesh, millions of former Pakistanis became Bangladeshis. The land of what is now Pakistan has lived through two bloody and bitter 'partitions' and we should honour those who belonged to those lands of pre-Partition India and contributed to independent Singapore, regardless of what they are labelled as now.

The dismemberment of 1971 actually turned Pakistan into a West Asian state until the 1990s, when Pakistanis slowly opened up to the economic miracle in Southeast Asia.

My own exposure to 'Singapore' came when a family business of handmade carpets moved to 'Singapore' immediately after the Japanese surrender. In a conversation with then-President S.R. Nathan, while serving as High Commissioner here, he remembered them being at Orchard Road.

The first people from the areas now constituting Pakistan — Sindh and Punjab — came to Singapore following the British annexation of their lands in 1843 and 1849, respectively.

The Sindhis arrived and primarily set up textile businesses in various regional towns, including Singapore. Others followed, seeking better opportunities. One such young man was Mohandas Detaram Mahbubani, who "made the brave decision to come to Singapore alone as a 13 year old orphan." Going back to Sindh during the war, he then married and returned in 1947. Little did he realise that his son, Kishore, born a year later, would grow up to become Singapore's best-known Sindhi.

Kishore served in the Foreign Office, rising to its highest ranks and making Singapore's case across the world, writing books and is now the Dean of the Lee Kuan Yew School of Public Policy, raising succeeding generations of public servants for Singapore and much of the Asian region. Perhaps only a few have done more to bring Singapore to the world stage.

In 2007, "it was a dream come true" when Kishore walked into his maternal home in Hyderabad, Sindh, for the first time. He found the experience so moving that in his keynote address at the 2008 World Sindhi Sembelan (Congress), he recommended that all Sindhis retrace their roots.

Murli Kewalram Chinrai came from a wealthy Hyderabad Sindhi family and migrated to Singapore in the early 1950s via India. He reminisced of the Partition times with me: "There was no trouble and we did not want to leave," adding, "They were doing very well in Hyderabad [Sindh]." He had just got married and his in-laws were paranoid regarding troubles they heard in Punjab, he told me some years back. One day, he said, his in-laws booked a train bogie, arrived in a panic and they just packed up and left. Mr. Chinrai's family are the principal investors behind Singapore-based Olam, one of the biggest commodity companies in the world. His contribution and that of the Sindhi community to philanthropy is second to none, not only in Singapore, but elsewhere too.

The Sindhis in Singapore formed their association as early as 1921. They are reportedly only about 2000 of them in Singapore, and yet because of their business acumen and standing, they are able to punch above their weight.

A good number of Punjabis, and that includes Sikhs, were brought into Singapore in the wake of the restoration of British rule at the end of World War II. These men were mostly employed in public services like the police, post offices, customs and other clerical work. These Punjabis included artisans, watchmen and small traders. This is the group of men who ensured the smooth running of services, even after Singapore's independence, and contributed to Singapore society. Most Muslims amongst them are known to have married mainly Malay women and assimilated into the local culture.

The Sikhs who have organised themselves for the promotion of their sports and culture are active in business, public services, the armed forces and also in academia in Singapore.

Amongst the academicians was the late K.S. Sandhu, the longest-serving (1972–1993) Director of the Institute of Southeast Studies. His pioneering role in understanding the regional environment for the newly independent Singapore is unmatched. Today, a major wing in the ISEAS building is named after him in order to remember his contributions.

Originally belonging to Sialkot, now in Pakistan, the Thakral family's chief Kartar Singh Thakral moved to Singapore in the 1950s when his father sent him here from Bangkok in order to open the company offices. Never looking back, the Thakral Group is now one of the major conglomerates in Singapore, with operations in 25 countries.

Karan Sing Thakral, a scion who manages the company's huge operations in Indonesia and India, is also the Chairman of the South Asia Business Group within the Singapore Business Federation. He helps business development between Singapore and South Asia, thus bringing communities together.

After serving a term as Singapore's Non-Resident High Commissioner to Sri Lanka, he is now designated as the Ambassador to Denmark. Karan also contributes by nurturing young entrepreneurs through the global technology network TiE, which he headed for some years.

The Thakrals believe that while they are growing their business, they will effectively but quietly continue to play a role in various community causes. The family remains a uniting force amongst the Punjabis in Singapore.

One of the pioneering Pakistanis who played a lasting role in Singapore was late mariner Captain Mohammad Jalaluddin Sayeed. In 1968, newly independent Singapore asked Pakistan for expertise to advise on the formation of a shipping company, which "the government neither wished to subsidise nor to give protection." Pakistan deputed Captain Sayeed, who returned after preparing his report. Convinced of his commitment and credentials, he was asked back to float and run the company Neptune Orient Lines (NOL). Within 2 months, NOL ships were at sea. It is now amongst the top five such companies in the world.

On his departure in 1973 for a United Nations assignment, then-Prime Minister Lee Kuan Yew personally acknowledged Captain Sayeed's "invaluable" services to the NOL.

In September 2005, two days after Captain Sayeed died, his wife Zareena received a hand-delivered message in Karachi, from ESM Mr. Goh Chok Tong, who had earlier served under Captain Sayeed. The ESM wrote, "Captain Sayeed laid the keel for NOL and built it up into a reputable international line for which Singapore will always be grateful. None of us had ever run a shipping line and Captain Sayeed was patient in teaching us the ropes. On a personal level, I will always cherish Captain Sayeed's friendship. He was kind and considerate. He was unselfish in passing on his knowledge and I learnt quite a few things from him. He was in my eyes the perfect gentleman." Captain Sayeed's contribution helps Singapore fly its flag across the oceans.

In 2006, recognising his "pioneering spirit and his contributions to NOL and the maritime industry in Singapore," the NOL established a scholarship for the Master of Science in Maritime Studies offered at the Nanyang Technological University.

Dr. Shahzad Nasim is a typical case of a young Pakistani man who came to Singapore as a student in 1972. With a Master's degree in Civil Engineering from the National University of Singapore in 1976, he joined Meinhardt, an Australian engineering company. He has now come to own it, relocating its headquarters to Singapore with offices in 42 countries of the world.

Dr. Nasim's organisation has worked on some of the most iconic structures of Singapore and abroad, like One Raffles Quay, Pontiac Marina, The Sail@Marina Bay (Singapore's tallest residential building), The Paragon, Wisma Atria, Vivo City and the world's largest shopping mall in Dubai. Truly, in a sense, he contributed in making Singapore iconic.

Dr. Nasim contributes regularly through his membership of many professional committees. In fact, being the largest contributor at the South Asian Diaspora Conventions, he works to unite the community globally.

Sajjad Akhtar is currently Chairman of the international board of PKF International and a managing partner at the PKF-CAP LLP, a chartered accountancy firm, and he came to Singapore in 1980 to work with Arthur Anderson. Sajjad's professional integrity is acknowledged by the number of cases in which his assistance and advice is sought by courts in Singapore. In addition to his outstanding professional services, Sajjad is recognised for his community and charity work through the Rotary Club, where he also served as president, and other organisations. For his contributions to the Singapore society, the President of Singapore awarded him the Public Service Medal in 2007.

Shaukat Aziz, who headed the Citibank private banking arm in the Asia–Pacific during the early 1990s, became the Prime Minister of Pakistan from 2004 to 2008 and is remembered for his work across the wider Singapore community.

Many Pakistanis have teamed up to support the Singapore Urdu Development Centre, offering classes in the Urdu language to children.

The Singapore–Pakistani Association (SPA), founded in 1948 as the Overseas Pakistani League, continues to play an effective role in helping charities that are focused on the education of deprived children, healthcare, helping weddings of orphan girls and many more such noble but lesser well-known activities.

The SPA's President, Sophie Sheikh, moved to Singapore in 1988. In 1997, Sophie joined Pertapis Children's Home for abused and neglected children, teaching and taking care of their emotional and physical needs. "I took the female centre under my wing and managed to gain SPA's support to accept Pertapis as their regular bursary," thus serving causes across different communities.

Others, like Saad Janjua and Anwar ul Haq, have represented Singapore in sports fields at the highest levels. Many more, like Mushahid Ali, now at the Rajaratnam School of International Studies, have had the honour of contributing as diplomats and adding to Singapore's intellectual capital.

Despite the trauma of divisions, the community blends well with others and continues to play its role in Singapore's growth.

President Nathan at the Pakistan Food Promotion (PFP) Week dinner 2008 at the Raffles, talking to Faisal Ashraf, son of the High Commissioner Sajjad Ashraf.

HC chatting with the Speaker Abdullah Taramugi at the PFP dinner 2007.

Presenting a specially designed gift hamper, with Singapore Merlion and Pakistani figures, to the Speaker.

Talking to Minister Liu at the PFP dinner 2008. Prof. Tan Tai Yong in the middle.

HC speaking at the PFP dinner 2007. Minister Masagos Zulkifli, then Sr. Parliamentary Secretary, on the HC's left.

Sajjad Ashraf served as High Commissioner of Pakistan to Singapore from July 2004 to December 2008, finishing his term as the Dean of Diplomatic Corps in Singapore.

On completion of his Pakistan Foreign Service career in December 2008, he was appointed as an Adjunct Professor at the Lee Kuan Yew School of Public Policy, National University of Singapore (NUS) — a position he continues to hold.

He served as an Advisor to Fullerton Financial Holdings — a wholly owned Temasek subsidiary from 2009 to 2010. Mr. Ashraf served as a Visiting Senior Research Fellow at the ISEAS — Yusof Ishak Institute from 2010–2013.

From 2009–2015 he served three yearly terms as a Consultant with the Institute of South Asian Studies, NUS. He is a Consultant with Gerson Lehrman Group, and Guidepoint Global, US based primary research and expert network services.

His postings at home and abroad have allowed him to work in a broad range of countries on political, security and economic issues both in bi-lateral and multi-lateral settings.

Mr. Ashraf holds a Master's degree in Political Science from Forman Christian College, Lahore and a Master's degree in Defence and Strategic Studies from National Defence University, Islamabad.

His commentaries and op-ed pieces are regularly published in Singapore, US, Australia, Hong Kong and UAE amongst other countries.

15 The History of Parsis in Singapore

Pesi B. Chacha

Singapore was a Crown Colony founded by Sir Stamford Raffles in 1819 and was used as a criminal settlement for the Indian convicts. The first Parsi in Singapore unfortunately was a convict by the name of Muncherjee. When he fell seriously ill in 1829, an Armenian, Aristarcus Sarkies, persuaded the Parsis in China to buy a burial place for Zoroastrians/Parsis in Singapore. A plot of land was bought in what is today the most prestigious banking area of Shenton Way from funds raised by Hong Kong Parsi traders. In 1848, more land was bought adjacent to it in order to build a bungalow as a Parsi Lodge for Parsi traders from China to rest and hold Zoroastrian religious ceremonies. In fact, Mr. Cawasji Shapoorji was the first Parsi to reside in the region in Penang in Malaysia, much before the convict Muncherjee in Singapore. His name is on the records of Lodge Napier No. 441 in 1832. There was also a Parsi burial ground, but no records are available.

More Parsis had started settling down in Singapore by the middle of the 19th century. Among them was Mr. Fromurzee Sorabji, who died in 1849. His son Cursetjee married an English lady and was a founding partner of Little Cursetjee & Co., which later became the well-known John Little & Co., eventually a subsidiary of Robinson's Departmental Store of Singapore. Cursetjee was one of the trustees of the burial ground. When his business did not thrive, his creditors tried unsuccessfully to obtain possession of the burial land and the adjoining bungalow. After his death, a part of the land had to be sold in order to meet the costs of the litigation.

Another Parsi who made a name in Singapore was Dunjibhoy Hormusji, who served on the Grand Jury in 1854. Around that time, one Mr. Cama of Byramjee Hormusjee Cama & Co. opened an English school on Tanjong Pagar Road. He ran this school at his own expense for many years, giving free education to the local Chinese and others.

In 1889, the property was named 'The Parsi Lodge Charity' and Mr. Pestonjee and Mr. Muncherjee were the first two trustees. The income from the trust was used for charity and the upkeep of the burial ground. The last two trustees were Nanab-hoy Framjee and Dadabhoy Rustomjee. When they decided to leave Singapore and settle in Mumbai, India, the Government of Singapore transferred the trust to the Mohammedan & Hindu Endowments Board.

Another prominent Parsi in the 19th century was Mr. Edaljee Khory, an advoc-ate and solicitor who came from London after being in Yangon, Myanmar, for 10 years. He had the distinction of having a Masonic Lodge named after him: Edulji Khory Lodge of Mark Master Masons No. 436, a Founder Master in 1891. He later returned to London.

Another well-known Parsi who came to Singapore in 1898 was Mr. Heerji Pestonji Kaka, manager of Mr. J.M. Osman, a timber merchant. Mr. Kaka started a Chinese newspaper, although he was an English scholar. In 1906, one Mr. Sorabji Kavasji became the editor of the *Eastern Daily Mail*, an English daily. Later, it was taken over by the Straits Press Syndicate and he became the editor and manager.

In 1903, Framroze was one of the few Parsis in Singapore. He started the Fram-roze aerated water factory. Mr. Navroji Mistri came in 1909 to work at the Singapore docks, and later joined Framroze as a partner. When they parted, Navroji started his own Phoenix Aerated Water Co., later branching into real estate and restaurants. His G.H. Café on Battery Road operated for many years. Mr. Pesi Davar came to Singapore in 1925 and initially worked for his cousin, Navroji Mistri. He had very good accounting and business skills and later worked with the local government. He weathered difficult times through the Japanese occupation, and after the war, launched his own business with another Parsi, Minoo Warden. He started Davar & Co. in Penang Lane where today stands the 'Dhoby Ghaut' MRT station. He went into shipping, paint and timber businesses that stretched to Malaysia. He, like his cousin Navroji Mistri, remained a bachelor. He had a trusted Parsi friend, Mr. Nariman Bhaghat, who had come to Singapore after the war from Iran. When Mr. Davar passed away on 14 September 1978, he donated S$50,000 to the Parsi Association and left a few million of the rest of his entire estate in trust for charitable and educational institutions to Hong Kong and Shanghai Bank trustees and Mr. Nariman Bhaghat. Even today, the income generated from the trust is disbursed annually for charitable and educational purposes. Unfortunately, this humble Parsi remained unrecognised even amongst the Parsis.

Davar's cousin Navroji, who had also come with a handful of rupees, died a millionaire in 1953. Before his death, he donated 1 million Singapore dollars to the Ministry of Health to build a Mistri Wing for children at the Singapore General Hospital. The road adjoining his factory was named Navroji Road and the one next to the Parsi burial ground was named Parsi Road. Another Parsi who lived in

Singapore for many years was Dr. Rustom Chapkhana. His son Sorab was the only Parsi known to have been born in Singapore before the Second World War.

After the Second World War, more Parsis came to Singapore. Behram Vakil came from China and was a pillar of support for the Parsis as the only priest for many years. Keki Medora and his wife Nergish came after the war and Nergish Medora was a well-known social worker for those afflicted with leprosy. Even in her 80s and until her death in May 2000, she continued to work on social projects. She was awarded the prestigious Public Service Star (Bintang Bakti Masharakat) by the Government of Singapore.

Mr. J. Namazie, a Persian who resided in Singapore, encouraged the Parsis to form the Parsi Association on 29 May 1954, which took over the management of the Parsi Lodge Charity from the Mohammedan and Hindu Endowment Board. Framroze became the founding President and Keki Medora the secretary. When Framroze passed away, Hormusji Mistri became the President of the association for several years. The burial ground in Parsi Road was acquired by the Government in April 1969. The money accrued from the requisition of the land (close to half a million Singapore dollars) was held in trust in the Parsi Lodge Charity. The burial ground was then moved to Tampines behind the Paya Lebar airport and later to its present location at Chua Chu Kang in the mid-1970s.

On 27 May 1969, at an EOGM of the association, it was resolved to pass the administration of the Parsi Lodge Charity to Public Trustee. Two members elected from the Parsi Community and one from the Parsi Association formed the Committee of Management to assist the Public Trustee. The first committee comprised Behram Vakil, Rutton Patel and Noshir Mistri. The income from the investment of the Parsi Lodge Charity was spent annually on the improvement and upkeep of the burial ground, religious ceremonies, scholarships for the Parsi children of Singapore and also of other communities and for deserving charitable causes in Singapore.

In the 1960s, more Parsis came to Singapore, and amongst them were Keki Vesuna, Noshir Mistry and Soli Setna. Mr. Setna became one of the directors of Neptune Oriental Line of Singapore and was a close colleague of Senior Minister Mr. Goh Chok Tong. Pesi and Piloo Chacha (both doctors) came to Singapore in 1967. Dr. Pesi Chacha started as a Lecturer and later became Professor and Head of the Department of Orthopaedic Surgery of the National University of Singapore. He was awarded Palmes Academiques Grade of Knight by the French Government in 1976 and Arris and Gale Memorial Lectureship of the Royal College of Surgeons of England in 1979 for his research work. From his personal donation to the National University of Singapore, the Pesi B. Chacha Lectureship for Spine and Scoliosis

Surgery was established in 2013. For his pioneering work in hand and microvascular surgery, he was awarded the Pioneer Hand Surgery Award by the International Federation of Societies for the Surgery of Hand (IFSSH) on 4 March 2013.

In the 1970s, even more Parsis came to Singapore, especially the airline pilots and flight engineers who joined the fast-growing Singapore Airlines. More than a dozen Parsi pilots flew SIA and Silk Air from the mid-1970s to date. Among them were Billy Antia and his family, Phil and Nergis Medora and their daughter Niloufer and son Jal, Suna and Rusi Kanga, Russi and Shrin Ghadiali, Dhun and Maya Daruwalla, Baji and Yvonne Kapadia, Adi and Mona Kapadia, Jamshed and Naju Marazban, Rusi and Zarin Cooper and Roshen and Jimmy Daruwalla, among many others. From a dozen in the old days, the Parsi community grew to nearly 100 in the late 1980s and 1990s. The Parsi community in Singapore now numbers about 300.

The newly arrived Parsis continued to contribute and achieve recognition in various fields. Dr. Jimmy Daruwalla (an orthopaedic surgeon) became the founding President of the Dyslexia Association of Singapore at its inception in 1991. Jamshed Medora (a chartered accountant) became Justice of Peace in 1994. He was awarded the Public Service Medal (Pingkat Bakti Masharakat) in 1991 and the Public Service Star (Bintang Bakti Masharakat) in 1993. Russi Ghadiali became the President of the Rotary Club in July 1995 and contributed significantly to the Inter-religious Organisation in Singapore and also to the renamed Parsi Zoroastrian Association of South East Asia (PZAS). He was also responsible for organising the 3000 Years of Zoroastrian Anniversary from 28 to 30 May 2004, which was graced by President Nathan. His wife Shirin was the first Parsi lady to be the President of the Inner Wheel Club of Singapore from 1998 to 1999, and their daughters Natasha (now a doctor) and Kharmayne were national gymnasts. Kharmayne is the only Parsi girl who has represented Singapore in gymnastics at five Southeast Asian Games and won a bronze medal. Jimmy Doctor became the President of the Lions Club in 1992. Zenobia Aspar was the first Parsi to be the President of Thomson Toastmaster's Club from 1995 to 1996 and the District Governor, Area S1, from 1997 to 1998. Rohan Bhappu was Singapore Junior Open Squash champion for under-16s in 1995 and for under-19s from 1996 to 1998, winning the Trinity Open Juniors in the USA in 1998. Zubin Shroff is the only Parsi cricketer who has represented the Singapore national team and has captained the national team.

On 18 March 2011, with encouragement from the Minister for Foreign Affairs, Mr. George Yeo and Mr. Gopinath Pillai, previously Ambassador to Iran, the President of the PZAS and Mrs. Dilnawaz Zaveri organised a Navroze function at the Orchard Hotel with the participation of the Iranian community in Singapore. President Nathan was the guest of honour.

Mr. Homiyar Vasania bought a shop house at 83 Desker Road from his own personal money in the memory of his late father on 18 April 2011, and leased it to the PZAS for a nominal monthly rental of S$1 per month as Zoroastrian House of the community for lectures and member interaction.

The Parsi community in Singapore will continue to grow, flourish and contribute to the development of Singapore. The Singapore Government recognises the Zoroastrian religion as one of the ten religions included under IRO and is aware of the contributions and achievements of this very small community in Singapore.

Dr. Pesi B. Chacha in the cockpit of Cessna 172 single engine aircraft at Seletar Airport. (This photograph was provided by Dr. Pesi B. Chacha for publication in *The Sunday Times*: November 15, 1998, for the article titled "A pilot for just 11 days, but it was worth it.")

Dr. Pesi B. Chacha in the cockpit of Cessna 172 single engine aircraft before taxiing and takeoff at the Seletar Airport. (This photograph was provided by Dr. Pesi B. Chacha for publication in *The Straits Times* Saturday, January 7, 2006, for an article titled "Flying high.")

Dr. Pesi B. Chacha after obtaining his PPL (Private Pilot License) just 11 days before his 60th birthday; standing in front of the aircraft Cessna 172 with his mentor and instructor, Mr. Darshan Singh. The aircraft initially belonged to the SIA Flying Club, later renamed Seletar Flying Club.

Dr. Pesi B. Chacha standing in front of the aircraft Cessna 172 which initially belonged to the SIA Flying Club, later renamed Seletar Flying Club.

Achnowledgements

I would like to specially acknowledge the late Mrs. Suna Kanga who had helped a lot in tracing the past history of the Parsis in Singapore. I also wish to thank all those members of the Parsi Community who helped in one way or the other to compile this history. Thanks once again for giving me this opportunity to showcase the contributions that the Parsi Community has made to the country that they have adopted as their own.

Pesi B. Chacha was born on 31 July 1938 in Navsari, one of the largest diamond polishing towns in the state of Gujarat in India. After his early childhood in the northern town of Lukhnow, his parents moved to Mumbai where he did his schooling at the Esplanade High School and St. Xavier Junior College. Although very keen on pursuing an engineering course, he decided to do medicine, encouraged by his mother. He studied at the Grant Medical College in Mumbai from 1955 to 1960, graduating with distinction and a gold medal in Obstetrics and Gynaecology. He did not accept the residency in obstetrics and gynaecology, having been inspired by his orthopaedic teachers Professors Masalawalla and Joshipura to do orthopaedics. He left for postgraduate studies in U.K. in February 1962. He obtained his Fellowships of the Royal College of Surgeons of Glasgow and Edinburgh in 1963 and 1965. He did his orthopaedic residency training at the University Teaching Hospital, Western Infirmary Glasgow under Professor Roland Barnes and did his M.Ch. Orth. at the University of Liverpool in 1966.

In November 1967 he joined the Department of Orthopaedic Surgery of the National University of Singapore as a lecturer under Professor V.K. Pillay. His main interests then were in scoliosis, hand surgery and limb lengthening in children. It was Prof. Pillay who encouraged him to take a special interest in scoliosis and start scoliosis clinics in the department. He was awarded M.D. by the National University of Singapore in December 1972 for his thesis on Experimental and Clinical work on "Autologous Composite Tissue Tendon Grafts for Division of Both Flexor Tendons in the Digital Theca of the Fingers."

He was promoted to Senior Lecturer in 1972, to Associate Professor in 1973 and to full Professorship in 1978. When Professor Pillay left for private practice in 1972, he became the head of the Orthopaedics Department. In 1976, he received the meritorious Palmes Academiques, Grade of Knight, French National Award by the French Government for his academic achievements. His interest in hand and reconstructive microsurgery took him to visit the world renowned micro-vascular surgeon, Professor Yoshi Ikuta in Hiroshima Japan in 1975. On his return with the aid of a generous donation by the Lion's Club of Singapore, an operating microscope and microsurgical instruments were bought to start pioneering work in microvascular surgery for the first time in South East Asia. Reattachment of amputated fingers, hands and arms from industrial accidents was now possible as well as resurfacing of large wounds and bridging of bone defects with microvascular flaps and bone grafts. With his colleague Professor Robert Pho, teaching workshops for microsurgery were conducted to train young surgeons in Singapore and the region. In recognition of this work and for conducting microsurgery workshops, he was awarded F.R.A.C.S. by the Royal Australasian College of Surgeons in February 1980 and the International Society of Reconstructive Microsurgery presented him an award in 1996 for Advancement of Reconstructive Microvascular Surgery in Singapore.

In April 1979 he was awarded the prestigious Arris and Gale Memorial Lectureship of the Royal College of Surgeons of England for his work on "Clinical and Experimental Study of Muscle Pedicle Transfer of Ipsilateral Fibula into the Tibia for Non-union of the Tibia with a Large Gap." At the same time he was the first Singaporean Orthopaedic Surgeon to be awarded the Visiting Professorship to U.K. by the Commonwealth Universities Interchange Scheme from 23 April to 19 May 1979.

In recognition of his interest in scoliosis he was elected as a member of the prestigious Scoliosis Research Society in U.S. in 1979.

On 4 March 2013 he received the Pioneer Hand Surgeon award from the International Federation of the Societies for the Surgery of Hand (IFSSH) as a pioneer hand surgeon from Singapore.

From his personal donation to the National University of Singapore, Pesi B Chacha Lectureship in Orthopaedic Surgery for advancement of Scoliosis and Spine Surgery was established from 2014 with the first overseas lecturer invited in January 2014. This is to continue on a yearly basis.

16 The Singapore Indian Community towards SG100

K. Kesavapany and Asad Latif

The story of Indian Singaporeans in the next 50 years begins on the high note struck 50 years ago. Singapore's founding fathers envisaged an integral national role for them born of rights and not sufferance. The enshrinement of Tamil as one of the four official languages was a reminder to all Singaporeans that Indians had an acknowledged place in the national scheme of things. To Indians, the message was that they would need to think and behave as Singaporeans first and last. Certainly, the ancestral part of their national identity was an important component of their personal and social consciousness, but ethnicity was not destiny: nationalism was and would be. Fifty years from 1965, Indian Singaporean children enjoy a confidence that is no less than that felt by children from other races, although Indians are Singapore's second minority. Indeed, one of Singapore's greatest achievements is that minority status confers protection, but does not invoke insecurity. From the protection of Tamil to the attempt to ensure minority representation in Parliament through the Group Representation Constituencies scheme, being from a minority community has its advantages. This is no small matter given the ways in which minorities elsewhere are sometimes turned into scapegoats for all that goes wrong with the national direction set by a jealous majority. Singapore must preserve this multiracial status quo into the next half-century.

As a minority, Indians are also beneficiaries of the meritocratic system that has enabled many members of the community to move to the top in politics, the civil service, the military, business, professions and civic life. That they have done so without ethnic reservations and quotas speaks highly of their ability. This system must be preserved at all costs. There is no success as precarious as one derived from positive discrimination, no matter how well-meaning such a system might be. There is always a lurking idea then that the minorities are benefitting at the expense of a more talented majority. The discontent this breeds gets reflected back at the minorities, robbing them of the right to say that they can and do compete on equal terms. Again, the experiences of other countries in this regard are instructive.

It is important not to forget pockets of under-achievement within the community in spite of the strides made by it as a whole — and equally, what the rest of the nation can do about such under-achievement. At The Crossroads, the 1991 Report of the Action Committee on Indian Education, noted: "While the community should primarily rely on its own resources to improve its well-being, the Committee believes that correcting the educational under-performance of any segment of Singaporeans is a national concern that merits the deployment of national resources, in Singapore's continued search for excellence and higher productivity." This deployment took the form of SINDA, which rightly identified education as one of the key challenges faced by Indians. Much has been done since SINDA's establishment in 1991, but challenges continue because of advances in technology and the general rise in educational standards nationally. Greater efforts are required to identify the under-performers among Indian youth and to find ways to help them realise their potential. For example, out of the 4000 Indian children who enter the educational system every year, only 800 make it to universities or polytechnics. The reasons for this gap must be found and addressed. What Mr. Piyush Gupta, the chief executive officer of DBS Group Holdings, said in the context of the bank's challenge in managing the new Internet world applies broadly to Indians as well: "If we don't respond suitably by digitising our own offerings, by re-imagining the customer's journey, and leveraging new technology to give them a differentiated experience, we are going to die."

Focusing on education would need to be matched by other measures to prevent an Indian underclass from forming and solidifying in the next few decades. Income inequality cannot be prevented in an open, globalised economy, but the social stagnation and stratification it produces can be ameliorated. Here, again, the effort is a national one — to help Indians not because of their ethnicity, but their nationality.

Overall, the key need would be to make the Indian community mainstream, particularly as national and intra-ethnic dynamics are affected by immigration. Arriving Indians have undoubtedly enriched the talent pool of the Indian community as a whole in various spheres, including banking, information technology and culture. However, they should not be viewed as a group apart, but as an integral part of the whole. This will occur over time, as it has occurred with the settled community. Efforts to integrate immigrants at the national level should be reflected at the community level as well. Indian Singaporeans must remain a confident part of the national fabric, their numbers bolstered by the new arrivals, but their national wavelength attuned to their long and distinguished presence in Singapore.

It is instructive to end with the remarks made by Minister Indranee Rajah at a gathering in Singapore in September 2015: "We just had our GE and that has set us in a direction which will take us towards Singapore's future, SG100. We cannot stop here and congratulate ourselves for how far we have come. We work for the next 50 years. The things that we do today, tomorrow and the next few years are going to determine the direction, the shape and the whole timbre of Singapore society and the way that we develop as a country for the next 50 years. It is a very exciting journey," she said. "The Indian community in particular has a very important role to play here. The Indian community has contributed much to [the richness and diversity] of society. The individuals in the Indian community have made several contributions in their own right as well as part and parcel of Indian organisations. And the Indian community as a whole has made Singapore richer for being part of Singapore..."

That journey must gain momentum.

Mr. K. Kesavapany was the Director of the Institute of Southeast Asian Studies, Singapore from October 2002 until 28th February 2012. Prior to this, he was Singapore's High Commissioner to Malaysia from 1997 to 2002. He also served as Singapore's Permanent Representative to the United Nation in Geneva and concurrently accredited as Ambassador to Italy and Turkey from 1991 to 1997. He was elected as the first Chairman of the General Council of the WTO when it was established in January 1995 and a member of the Singapore Mediation Centre's International Panel of Mediators.

Mr. K. Kesavapany graduated from the University of Malaya with a Bachelor of Arts (Honours) degree and obtained a Master of Arts (Area Studies) degree from the School of Oriental and African Studies, University of London.

Mr. Kesavapany is Singapore's Non-Resident Ambassador to the Hashemite Kingdom of Jordan.

Mr. Kesavapany is a Distinguished Affiliated Fellow, Asian Research Institute, National University of Singapore, Governor on the Board of the Singapore International Foundation and President of the Singapore Indian Association (SIA).

Asad Latif came from India to Singapore in 1984 to work as a journalist, first for *The Business Times* and then for *The Straits Times*. He took his Honours in English at Presidency College, Kolkata, and read History at Clare Hall, Cambridge, where he was a Chevening (Raffles) and an S. Rajaratnam Scholar. He was a Jefferson Fellow at the East-West Center and a Fulbright Visiting Scholar at Harvard.

Index

www.ingramcontent.com/pod-product-compliance
Lightning Source LLC
Chambersburg PA
CBHW080647270326
41928CB00017B/3218